Work On Your Game Inc.
1300 Washington Ave #153
Miami Beach FL 33119

A Message About Why We Created This Booklet

Thanks for taking the time to read this booklet!

We created it to give you a sampling of what our clients have said about working with, learning from and being coached by Dre Baldwin over the years.

Full Disclaimer: Dre has been "in the game" since 2005. If we published ALL of the feedback we've gathered from clients, customers and viewers since then, this booklet would be well north of 1,000 pages.

So our compromise was to gather some of the most pertinent things that give you a clear picture of what Dre is about, who he helps and how he helps them without overwhelming you with too much.

We hope what you're about to read is informative for you!

Work On Your Game Inc.
#WorkOnYourGame

Work On Your Game Inc.
1300 Washington Ave #153
Miami Beach FL 33119

What Clients Say About Dre Baldwin & Work On Your Game

A small sampling of feedback and comments we've gotten from the people we've had the privilege to serve here at Work On Your Game Inc….

I Would Sometimes Let [Lack Of] Self-Confidence Get In My Way…

Dre helped me get my mind right and become the person who I wanted to be. I highly recommend Dre for anyone who wants to to get on the path of getting your mind right and achieving the things that you really want to do. Work On Your Game!

- John Madson, Financial Advisor, Minneapolis, Minnesota

Takes Complex Issues And Builds A Roadmap in Reverse…

I knew it was time for me to get serious about the changes I wanted to make with myself, and from following [Dre's] work I knew he was the person who would be real and direct with me… I really appreciate his help.

- Chad Weigle, Financial Advisor, Dixon, Illinois

Added Staff and Freed Up Hours

Thanks to Dre's advice, I've added staff to my academy and turned over management to delegate responsibility. I am able to deliver on the same time I was allocating to just one task before. I just needed to take that first step of faith. It's getting easier and now I continue to expand my capacity.

- Rob Pierson, Basketball Academy Owner & Coach, Broomfield, Colorado

Work On Your Game Inc.
1300 Washington Ave #153
Miami Beach FL 33119

You Have Really Motivated Me

I want to thank you for the opportunity to open my awareness and thank you for the motivation. I just built my tea company in China here in the tea gardens of Wuyi mountain. I would like to express my sincere gratitude to you. I still remember your powerful talk. It has really motivated me. Here I am and I would like to say thank you.

- Peiqin Zhao, Business Owner, Wuiyi, China

No Sugar Coating Here!

Reality can be harsh making the truth hard to face sometimes; I love that Dre is a straight shooter and shares his insight where it's black and white. He has a wide array of topics that are Very relatable for just about anyone — a must listen to!!!

- Stefanie Johnson, Professional Bowler, McKinney, Texas

Organize All The Moving Parts Of Your Life…

Dre has a great program for you, regardless of what you do, and helps you prioritize the things you ought to be focused on. Dre's approach is honest with clear communication that's easy to understand. He has a lot to offer for anyone who wants to make changes in their life.

- Kevin Hodges, DoD Business Owner & U.S. Military Veteran Triangle, Virginia

Work On Your Game Inc.
1300 Washington Ave #153
Miami Beach FL 33119

I Am So Incredibly Grateful… You're The Best

Dre, The life I decided to create when we talked is coming into being every day. It's all coming together like you said! Thank you for changing my course by pushing me and challenging me. I honestly don't think I could have heard it from anyone but you at that point.

- Jean South, Military Veteran & Business Owner, Jacksonville, Florida

A Tough, Truth-Telling Coach

Dre is a tough, truth-telling coach who can change your game by teaching you how to work on it in the right ways. None of what he shares is easy, but all of it is smart, and if you have the guts to do the work, this book will show you the path to success.

- Nick Morgan, Bestselling Author, Boston, Massachusetts

Cannot Thank You Enough For Being As Real As Possible

*… Everything changed. I went in every morning charged and motivated. [You] pushed me to have bigger ambition and a 'no excuses' attitude which became the way I organically operate today. You helped me realize my potential, my talent, what drives me. Taught me to f*** the excuses, opinions and the norm. I left that job, and started my own business. 3 months in and I am constantly turning down clients because there simply are too many! I wake up driven, excited and charged every single day. Keep doing what you're doing.*

- Tania Jeyda, Interior Designer & Business Owner, Gold Coast, Australia

Work On Your Game Inc.
1300 Washington Ave #153
Miami Beach FL 33119

Added Tremendous Value To My Life

I have known Dre for years now, and every interaction I have with him adds tremendous value to my life. From sitting down with him 1-on-1 to discussing the next steps for my business, the wisdom and guidance he shares has always been on-point, visionary and empowered. Thank you, Dre, for the contribution you are to so many lives on this planet. You rock!

- Jeska Brodbeck, Mindful Performance Coach, Miami Beach, FL

I Went From Good To Unstoppable

I was a really good basketball player physically but mentally I wasn't there... I went from good to unstoppable. Dre doesn't just cover Confidence. He covers Confidence, discipline, Visioning Success, dealing with negativity, mindset mistakes and much, much more! I have recommended Dre to anyone who wants to be serious in basketball or anything in life. Thank you again and Work On Your Game!

- Grayson Honaker, College Athlete, Wise, Virgina

A Great Resource For Coaching Basketball…

Just finished the book over the weekend—thanks so much for all the great info. It will be a great resource coaching at a Div 3 school---I know our best player from this season is trying to continue to play. Looking forward to sharing the info—great thoughts on mental toughness. Thanks again,

- Brad Oringer, College Basketball Coach, Brookly, NY

Work On Your Game Inc.
1300 Washington Ave #153
Miami Beach FL 33119

Your Words Of Confidence Had The Greatest Impact On Me And Helped Me Achieve Today's Victory!

I would like to thank you for your words of hope and to say that I passed the exam and I'm already a lawyer. It was your words of confidence that had the greatest impact and helped me to overcome defeat and to continue working to achieve today's victory! God bless you!

- Lili, Lawyer, South Florida

My Mental Game Has Grown In Strength And It Shows!

Your podcast came up in the suggestions – I gave one a try and I've been hooked since! It helps get my mind right and reinforce everything that I am doing :)The rodeo world is very different in many aspects from other athletics. So when doing something different from the status quo, the naysayers grow. But since listening my mental game has grown in strength and it shows!

- **Kaylee Smith, Rodeo Competitor, Wyoming**

An Immediate Improvement

Been hearing compliments all day about your presentation. It really resonated with the audience. One of the attendees teaches dance part-time. She used some of your ideas at her class last night. It had to do with switching partners around. She actually saw an immediate improvement in one of her dancers.

- Jim Miller, Senior Director, Maryland HHRA

You're Changing Lives Out Here!

I appreciate your advice and will be following what you said today. I'm one of your avid daily listeners (and one of your actual appliers of advice) and have ALREADY started to ask those initial questions to potential clients. You're changing lives out here man, I hope you know and understand that.

- Jasmine Kearse, Creative Consultant, Brookly, NY

Work On Your Game: Get to it!

Practical, useful and urgent advice from someone who's been in your shoes. There's work to be done, get to it.

- **Seth Godin, Bestselling Author Of This Is Marketing And Tribes**

…Used It To Play Overseas

I am an avid listener of your podcast. I made it overseas last year after overcoming a lot of closed doors. I used a lot of your material to guide me through the process and to get a taste of what to expect. Also, your podcast about reading books impacted my life in a huge way. I want to thank you for the material you put out. Keep up the great, quality work!

- Raychel Shannon, Pro Athlete & Business Owner, New York

Work On Your Game Inc.
1300 Washington Ave #153
Miami Beach FL 33119

"I have been listening to you for a while now and you've opened up my eyes a lot as a person and made me more competitive as a basketball player. Thank you so much for everything that you do. Much love and respect." **- Mahmoud Abdelhamid**

"Thank you (and the team?) for what you do. You're changing lives for the better. I'd guess that you're getting enough feedback at this point that mine but I'm taking the time anyways because the messages you produce and publish are worthy of it. I downloaded itunes and signed up for an apple id to post a review this morning after listing to your most recent episode #802 How To Pay Less Attention To What Others Are Doing. It is a little religious experience to wake up obsessing over something useless only to turn over in bed, to grab a podcast to quiet the demons, and to be greeted by something so directly relevant to the things I am struggling with. You're doing good things and I hope you keep it up." **– Blue Newman**

"Dre is a master of peeling back the layers to get to what's really important. This book is a real, raw, and practical guide for getting whatever it is that you want. Be prepared to leave your excuses behind and experience mega growth." **- Misty Buck**

"I don't often get into motivational/coaching shows because they are full of taglines and jargon. Dre is different. There are real gems here." **- Musicbred**

"I've been following Dre's content since 2017 and he has given out one consistent thing in his content, HONEST TRUTH. It's not sugar cooked, Dre is not a yes man, he's not going to tell you what you want to hear, he's going to tell you what you NEED to hear. You may not agree with it, you may not even like it, but you will hear the truth from Dre in all of his content. It's really up to you on how you decide to consume the truth. #WorkOnYourGame.." **- Sabali**

"It's insane how these topics are SPOT ON and RELATABLE. Dre's advice is also ACTIONABLE Dre has helped me with the following, How to keep going when you're seeing little to no results, How to keep going when things aren't going your way, How to make noise in the beginning of your journey and how to get in front of people who will pay you for your service and product. Applicable, actionable, and real stuff no bluff" **- Justin**

"Dre Baldwin speaks to my heart and inspires me!! He speaks directly with no fluff to help people help themselves. This podcast, if you apply Dre's principles to how they are applicable to your life, will give you a 100% ROI on the investment in your time. Very grateful I found this podcast and how it has helped me to improve my life." **- Drea**

"I love Dre Baldwin's podcast. He gives great ideas and tips, it's organized, practical (you can put it to use right away), and delivered at a quick pace. Dre is a very engaging and authentic speaker. I recommend him all the time to my friends, clients, and family. Check him out, you'll be impressed!" **- Kimberly**

"If you're looking for a podcast that is real and doesn't waste time, this is it. Dre gets right to the point with information that can help you in any area of your life. Check it out!" **- Tim**

"I find Mr Baldwin's podcast to be like listening to a friend, neighbor or coworker telling me the real deal. His style connects with me and gets me fired up. I wish I could maintain the energy level I get from listening to his podcast throughout the day." **- REI Dad**

"Only took one episode for me to know that Dre's the real deal—already recommended this podcast to my buddy trying to make my college's basketball team and my entrepreneur friend."

"My #1 Go-To Show for All Things Mindset!
I thoroughly enjoy Dre Baldwin's podcast not just because his content is so methodically produced & well thought out...
But also because his messages provide actionable insights I can use to hone my game day in and day out.
Anyone who's looking to improve their personal productivity through action—not fluff—will enjoy Dre's podcast.
What I enjoy most about #WOYG is its coming from a guy who has and IS living out what he's discussing as opposed to promoting hype.
Last, lemme just say I appreciate Dre's 'what you see is what you get' persona because that shows he truly cares about his audience." **- Benin Brown**

"Best show on motivation This is the best show to listen to first thing in the morning to get your mind right and set you on a good path for the day ahead and I love Dre's delivery!" **- Brooklyn Gial**

"Dre is a professional in what he does. I've learned from him for many years. He's a great communicator and excels in teaching personal development, business principles and anything regarding basketball too.

He always has value to add to the content space and continues to do so day in and day out. His consistency combined with his content is outstanding. Keep it up Dre." **- PariGhai**

"I'm a "newer" subscriber to this show and just in the 10-15 episodes I've heard so far I'm blown away! Love the way he gets the message across and it helps me stay motivated! It's not the typical "raw raw" motivational stuff I'm used to hearing. Rather, Dre uses his personal experiences and life stories to help teach others and that to me is super important. Must listen podcast right here!!"

"This is my go to podcast when I want to motivate and refocus myself on my goals. I'd recommend it to anyone devoted to reaching new levels of improvement." **- TheKoMax**

"Dre Baldwin will tell you exactly what you need (not want) to hear. He's here to help us get over ourselves and our limiting belief system in order to BE a true professional in our area of expertise, then to start DOING what a professional must do in order to win, and finally to HAVE what a professional has as a result of putting in the work and delivering on his commitments over an extended period of time. Work on My Game!" **- Henry Neilsen**

"I have been tuned in to this podcast for about a year and a half now and I can honestly say I love the range of topics he covers as well as his style of putting it to you straight! If you want to improve yourself this is the only podcast you need to listen to! You won't regret it!" **- CMWeigle**

Work On Your Game Inc.
1300 Washington Ave #153
Miami Beach FL 33119

"Fresh, sharp and driven perspectives
I love this content and what Dre does in general because every time I think I know where he's going with the title he brings a new, fresh element to the equation. He relates thought processes and life tactics across many sectors of life which is awesome. This show also makes you feel like a part of a bigger group of driven, go-getters who aspire to change their lives for the better through many values tied into the WOYG podcast. Thank you Dre!" **– Leek Lemke**

"I've been listening to Dre for years for basketball help but recently began frequently listening to the work on your game podcast in order to improve my life and it has helped me substantially in succeeding towards reaching my goals through teaching me the mental discipline and giving me life lessons and ways to look at life in positive ways in order to reach my goals in basketball and in life.
I'm a big fan Dre" **- Daniel Gospodinov**

"Changes my life
As an independent videographer and mentor to at risk youth this podcast has helped me with the skills to go from a ineffective leader to a strategic leader . The tips and conversations are very realistic and take life for what it is . I wish I had taken this podcast seriously at a young age . Do not miss his chance." **- Loretta Lyn**

Work On Your Game Inc.
1300 Washington Ave #153
Miami Beach FL 33119

★★★★★
Musicbred, 02/06/2022
Great find!
I don't often get into motivational/coaching shows because they are full of taglines and jargon. Dre is different. There are real gems here. I wish Apple would put the old epi... more

★★★★★
Joshj1140, 12/23/2021
Dre always delivers
Been listening a long time. By far my favorite podcast.

★★★★★
Lgrubaugh, 12/10/2021
No victims here!
Love the No Victims Here!

★★★★★
glossa1995, 10/20/2021
Very beneficial
Practical, applicable knowledge for all aspects of life.. Thank you Dre.

★★★★★
The Sabali Podcast.., 09/11/2021
The HONEST truth..
I've been following Dre's content since 2017 and he has given out one consistent thing in his content, HONEST TRUTH. It's not sugar cooked, Dre is not a yes man, he's not g... more

★★★★★
ayyeeejustin, 08/04/2021
Dre is the ONLY person who's spot on in th...
It's insane how these topics are SPOT ON and RELATABLE. Dre's advice is also ACTIONABLE Dre has helped me with the following, How to keep going when you're seeing little to... more

★★★★★
lady_drea, 06/15/2021
100% ROI
Dre Baldwin speaks to my heart and inspires me!! He speaks directly with no fluff to help people help themselves. This podcast, if you apply Dre's principles to how they are... more

★★★★★
LJones01, 06/05/2021
Great lessons for business, sports and life
Dre always delivers powerful and practical advice in a straightforward way. He's the big brother or coach you need.

★★★★★
Ay Rod, 05/17/2021
Appreciate you
Thank you for showing up everyday and giving us game.

★★★★★
JCL2, 05/14/2021
Short, sweet, to the point: get off your beh...
I love Dre's direct approach. He has motivated me to take action, to *work less*, to *show up more*, and to be *myself* more.
His books are full of actionable content... more

★★★★★
Kimberly, is that you?, 05/08/2021
Terrific podcast!
I love Dre Baldwin's podcast. He gives great ideas and tips, it's organized, practical (you can put it to use right away), and delivered at a quick pace. more

★★★★★
Lil genki, 04/04/2021
WOYFG
I have been listening to this podcast consistently for years now, and I'm still enlightened every single episode. No better place to be if you're aiming to improve... more

★★★★★
Tim, NC, 03/29/2021
Cuts to the chase
If you're looking for a podcast that is real and doesn't waste time, this is it. Dre gets right to the point with information that can help you in any area of your life. Check it out!

★★★★★
BV150, 03/24/2021
Great
The best podcast out there if you are serious about your game, Dre does an awesome job at getting his points across in a very easy way to understand and breaks everything down... more

★★★★★
REI Dad, 03/18/2021
Motivating
I find Mr Baldwin's podcast to be like listening to a friend, neighbor or coworker telling me the real deal. His style connects with me and gets me fired up. I wish I could maintain... more

★★★★★
PS696, 03/03/2021
Review
Dre shares more than just information, and, knowledge, he shares insight and wisdom.

★★★★★
A bad app, 02/15/2021
Real deal
Only took one episode for me to know that Dre's the real deal—already recommended this podcast to my buddy trying to make my college's basketball team and my... more

★★★★★
Benin brown, 02/08/2021
My #1 Go-To Show for All Things Mindset!
I thoroughly enjoy Dre Baldwin's podcast not just because his content is so methodically produced & well thought out...
more

Work On Your Game Inc.
1300 Washington Ave #153
Miami Beach FL 33119

⭐⭐⭐⭐⭐
abiolang, 01/09/2021

Awesome
Thank you for all you put out here... it has really changed me into a better person.

⭐⭐⭐⭐⭐
Brooklyn Gial, 12/31/2020

Best show on motivation
This is the best show to listen to first thing in the morning to get your mind right and set you on a good path for the day ahead and I love Dre's delivery!

⭐⭐⭐⭐⭐
G4M3R-4-R34L, 12/31/2020

How????
How am I just now hearing about this podcast smh 😩. Dre breaks down everything he talks about to bacon bits so you can really understand it & begin to apply it to your   more

⭐⭐⭐⭐⭐
Bonnie Frank, 12/29/2020

Episode #1690 is a MUST listen
Listening to Dre's episode #1690 and why social media isn't truly free was packed with knowledge bombs. This eye opening episode should be heard by everyone.

⭐⭐⭐⭐⭐
vmi2002, 12/26/2020

Effective, Inspiring, and Actionable
It's clear how inspirational he is and how he is a 4x Ted speaker.

⭐⭐⭐⭐⭐
stefaniebbeauty, 12/18/2020

Love this for motivation and good info
Just found this and I am binge listening! Definitely gave me some good info and motivates me to push harder

⭐⭐⭐⭐⭐
Senile Sapien, 11/21/2020

5/5
Thank you for the useful information. You are a great guidance to us all.

⭐⭐⭐⭐⭐
Adafafaga, 11/19/2020

Helps me out a ton
I'm a 21 y/o college student and I started following Dre when he was doing basketball videos now I listen to the podcast everyday at work and it's a big help!!

⭐⭐⭐⭐⭐
BBC gunner, 11/10/2020

Mr. Consistent!
Dre is a professional wordsmith. He's well versed in a variety of different topics.

⭐⭐⭐⭐⭐
PariGhai, 03/13/2020

Excellent
Dre is a professional in what he does. I've learned from him for many years. He's a great communicator and excels in teaching personal development, business principles and   more

⭐⭐⭐⭐⭐
Biggest Fan 208, 02/26/2020

So freaking good!!
I'm a "newer" subscriber to this show and just in the 10-15 episodes I've heard so far I'm blown away! Love the way he gets the message across and it helps me stay   more

⭐⭐⭐⭐⭐
TheKoMax, 01/31/2020

Best Podcast for Growth in Life
This is my go to podcast when I want to motivate and refocus myself on my goals. I'd recommend it to anyone devoted to reaching new levels of improvement.

⭐⭐⭐⭐⭐
AwesomeAce18, 01/28/2020

The Best
This is my go to podcast. He puts up a great one every morning, lots of good information for athletes and everyone else. Thanks Dre!

⭐⭐⭐⭐⭐
Henry Nielsen, 01/12/2020

Listen to this Daily!
Dre Baldwin will tell you exactly what you need (not want) to hear.
He's here to help us get over ourselves and our limiting belief system in order to BE   more

⭐⭐⭐⭐⭐
Demi.27, 01/04/2020

Life Changer
This podcast is one of the best podcasts I've ever listened to. Thank you Dre for the content.

⭐⭐⭐⭐⭐
coachgibbsmbb, 12/30/2019

Coach Gibbs
Love these Podcast!!

⭐⭐⭐⭐⭐
nobodycaresgolift, 12/04/2019

Woyg
This guy is hitting on points that you NEED to hear, topics that your GOING to experience and the way to get through these situations. Valuable life info

⭐⭐⭐⭐⭐
Samuel1111111111, 12/01/2019

Best Podcast out there!
He really know how to motivate, teach, preach, and release the right materials to get everyone in sports and the world of business. Recommended to everyone.

Work On Your Game Inc.
1300 Washington Ave #153
Miami Beach FL 33119

★★★★★
Cmweigle, 12/01/2019

If you want the truth…
I have been tuned in to this podcast for about a year and a half now and I can honestly say I love the range of topics he covers as well as his style of putting it to you straight! If y… more

★★★★★
art704, 11/25/2019

Great guy great motivational podcast
Big fan of Dre Baldwin, someone who has help me in my life to become mentally tough and strong.

★★★★★
johnoverturf, 11/10/2019

Good guy and good podcast!
Been watching his YouTube videos since I was young and just started listening to his podcasts. I love how his combines basketball with business, both my passions. Would… more

★★★★★
Gundogz, 11/08/2019

Great daily discipline tips
Dre breaks down everything you need to be the most confident person you can.

★★★★★
Leek Lemke, 11/06/2019

Fresh, sharp and driven perspectives
I love this content and what Dre does in general because every time I think I know where he's going with the title he brings a new, fresh element to the equation. He … more

★★★★★
Daniel_Gospodinov23, 10/31/2019

Excellent information!!!
I've been listening to Dre for years for basketball help but recently began frequently listening to the work on your game podcast in order to improve my life and it has helpe… more

★★★★★
Yeaidomythangbitchwhatsupp, 10/31/2019

Great motivating podcast
This podcast has helped me everyday to continue to better myself and be better everyday. Very well explained and easy to understand and apply instantly. Definite… more

★★★★★
StefanieNation11, 10/25/2019

Matter of fact
Love listening! Every topic is very relatable and I appreciate the real life insight an examples often shared.

★★★★★
loretta lyn, 10/12/2019

Changes my life
As a independent videographer and mentor to at risk youth this podcast has helped me with the skills to go from a ineffective leader to a strategic leader . The tips and conversa… more

★★★★★
spike no lee, 10/12/2019

Dre is the man
Dre never fails. I tune in everyday. ❗🙏

★★★★★
Jonathan Desir, 10/09/2019

How does this not have more views?
This is the greatest, most consistent podcast I've ever listened to. Having all this information when I'm young will certainly benefit me in the future. Dre not only sp… more

★★★★★
Debovalencia, 10/09/2019

Jump in anytime!
One of the best aspects about Dre's podcast is you can jump in anytime. You don't need to listen from #1 to catch up. Each one is clear and easy to understand. And they keep… more

★★★★★
King Official👏, 09/19/2019

Keep hittin em with those factz
Listen if you want good solid useful information. This is the brother to check out on his podcasts! I've been listening to him now for at least a month I follow and … more

★★★★☆
919 nicolas, 10/06/2019

Mr. Nicolas
Great podcast

★★★★★
2Banderas, 09/14/2019

Thank you Dre 🙏 Priceless!!
I truly appreciate your podcast, It has helped Tremendously. It feels that big brother still alive Every time I listen to it🙏. Please keep getting better I wish you nothing but su… more

★★★★★
Coach Stephens, 09/13/2019

Excellence!!!
Dre's podcast is amazing! It's one of the realest podcasts that definitely puts everything in perspective. I can honestly say that it's helped me hold myself accounta… more

★★★★★
Qwertyuioplkhgfdsa, 08/18/2019

Legit Value
This was my first time ever listening to his podcast, and the one I listened to was "Thinking is a Skill" — I'm currently on the path of self development trying to Work… more

★★★★★
beachboyt, 07/28/2019

Amazing
Speaking facts on so many levels! So many people need to here this! I just started listening and the podcast I have listened to have been amazing. I listened to the go… more

Work On Your Game Inc.
1300 Washington Ave #153
Miami Beach FL 33119

⭐⭐⭐⭐⭐
Seated Ambulator, 07/20/2019

Simply THE BEST OUT THERE!
This podcast is the best thing on the market today! Dre brings it every single day.

Dre takes the myriad concepts for succe... more

⭐⭐⭐⭐⭐
Rishab9093, 07/08/2019

Amazing
Daily motivation isn't something simply external, but it comes when you take yourself there mentally everyday. This podcast is big on helping you get there and allowing yo... more

⭐⭐⭐⭐⭐
Ellyson_Ortega, 06/20/2019

Best podcast ever!!!
This dude literally delivers every single day! He has not missed since the day he started the podcast which was somewhere around 2016! Dude is the definition of consisten... more

⭐⭐⭐⭐⭐
LordMcAllister, 06/15/2019

5 stars for Dre!
Best podcast for confidence (most important factor in life). Concise, actionable, competent, effective.

⭐⭐⭐⭐⭐
BP87!, 06/01/2019

No sugarcoating here!
I love the energy and real talk, straight to the point no BS. Great information and very motivational. Dre just has that Boise that makes you say, hell yeah I'm doing this now!!

⭐⭐⭐⭐⭐
1900hustler, 05/23/2019

💯💯💯
Great content everyday! Get your daily dose of WOYG

⭐⭐⭐⭐⭐
Mize777, 05/13/2019

Simple and effective!
I love this guy. He keeps it real and he keeps it simple. Give it a listen. I would bet that you give it a second listen and a third and a forth...

⭐⭐⭐⭐⭐
.ghrghgtnhthyrhrhgrhyrhryh, 05/12/2019

Dre keeps it 3 more than 97!
I have been quietly following Dre for over 10 years. He has shown a steady progression in the quality of content that he creates.
more

⭐⭐⭐⭐⭐
Elgin Frye, 05/01/2019

Thank You
I appreciate the knowledge you give me in Basketball as well as LIFE! WORK on Your GAME!

⭐⭐⭐⭐⭐
joo2h, 04/29/2019

You need to listen to this daily
This podcast will give you information that will help change your mindset when it comes to your everyday life. It has help me develop a growth mindset that has set me up for... more

⭐⭐⭐⭐⭐
Next GOAT NBA Player, 04/25/2019

Life changer
Have been listening for 2 years, dude changed my life.

⭐⭐⭐⭐⭐
College Hooper, 04/17/2019

He knows what he talking about
There are not too many people out there with the wealth of experience and skills that Dre possesses in life-skills/empowerment. Dre's background/journey as a former profess... more

⭐⭐⭐⭐⭐
nick aka beast mode, 04/14/2019

Improve yourself personal development
Best podcast ever Dre all day helps improve yourself aka ur game evey detail of your game

⭐⭐⭐⭐⭐
coats jaylan, 04/13/2019

Work on your game
If you want to be the best at what you do he is the man that can get you there🏀

⭐⭐⭐⭐⭐
drob1782, 04/02/2019

1st Time
First time listening to your podcast, look forward to the next episode!!! The real life advice given is beneficial to anyone.

⭐⭐⭐⭐⭐
FtLaudyFred, 03/28/2019

Love it!!!
I always look forward to the podcasts and I love the new book, Work On Your Game. I highly recommend it!

⭐⭐⭐⭐⭐
Blak One, 03/26/2019

Dre is the Way
I just started listening to Dre's podcasts and I thoroughly enjoy them. His frank and honest approach is refreshing.

⭐⭐⭐⭐⭐
Abby12908, 03/21/2019

A game changer
I just want to thank this podcast for improving my life. I struggled with low confidence most of my life. After listening to a few episodes, my confidence is back. His to the point... more

Work On Your Game Inc.
1300 Washington Ave #153
Miami Beach FL 33119

★★★★★
pogiboi619, 03/20/2019

Quality
Dre all day! Literally! The wisdom in these podcast makes me want to work on my game . In my sport and life .

★★★★★
Izzy00000, 03/20/2019

Listen every morning
I am new to this podcast but omg I do not start my morning without this. Dre has an energy and directness that makes me reflect on my own actions and how I internalize   more

★★★★★
LanguageDude, 03/08/2019

Amazing Podcast!
This podcast is a great one for sport players. I'm a struggling sophmore playing basketball, and it's a bit difficult to play at my peak performance, but this podcast reviews   more

★★★★★
durag lou, 02/18/2019

Great podcast
I started listening to dre podcast in 2016 since then this podcast has help with dealing success, work life, relationships, selfcare, personal investment and setback this is   more

★★★★★
bobo2298, 02/15/2019

WOYG
Listen to Dre every time I'm in the car, this guy does an amazing job of describing things in detail and giving examples. He keeps it all the way real

★★★★★
TonyManuDuncan, 02/12/2019

The BEST
Insightful, detailed, intelligent & at times funny!! Love this podcast! I'm a daily listener. Been following DreAllDay for literally decades, from YouTube videos, websites   more

★★★★★
pSUcoschw, 01/29/2019

PSUCoachW
This content is unreal. I'm a college basketball coach and listen everyday. It's great because you don't have to be a athlete to get great value. Keep bring that 🔥🔥

★★★★★
steve_mares13, 01/28/2019

Great content!!
Dre keeps it real and pushes you to be the best in any arena you could potentially be in! He's been a mental coach regarding my current situation; getting ready for my   more

★★★★★
🙏🙏👌, 01/25/2019

💯💯💯

★★★★★
Emily121199, 12/10/2018

Gives the best advice
This is by far my favorite podcast. He's real with you and knows what he's talking about.

★★★★★
Mar_214, 11/27/2018

Top podcast
Very inspirational podcast with 0 drop offs from each episode, you will think of ideas you may have previously looked over to better your life.. good daily listen for young people

★★★★★
KhalilGotYayo, 11/16/2018

Dre Got Game
Look man Dre got me doing something I have never done. Self evaluating. Very needed.

★★★★★
AndrewLaB, 11/11/2018

Vital to my morning routine.
Dre's intro sums it up greatly. This is a show that provides you with personal initiative or the 'go getter energy' every single day.

★★★★★
Ninjjata, 10/13/2018

Dre Is an Empowerment Guru!
Listen Dre doesn't just have all steer knowledge on hand, professional and real empirical information Dre pumps out. This is real talk" for this generation of motivate   more

★★★★★
Stev Collum, 09/16/2018

Dre All Day!
Free Jewel!!! used to follow your YouTube videos and now I'll be listening to every podcast. A lot more people need to hear your message. God bless your ministry broth   more

★★★★★
Zack Goldstein, 09/12/2018

The Best Motivational Speaker ALIVE
Dre Baldwin has a special talent when it comes to motivational speeches or in any speech. He will give u the confidence and mental strength u need to become the p   more

★★★★★
martenas godfrey, 09/03/2018

Dre all day, everyday, is essential audio en...
The title of my review suggests its entertainment, but thats only due to a lack of words to describe this. This is simply essential listening; a tool that is to be sharpened   more

★★★★★
angel_5245, 08/27/2018

The best
Dre has helped me become successful, this is a must listen

Work On Your Game Inc.
1300 Washington Ave #153
Miami Beach FL 33119

★★★★★
Hidingz, 07/25/2018

Best Podcast
Best Podcast I've heard on here well that I've listened too

★★★★★
jay-sc, 07/21/2018

Well done.
See is an impressive young man. Looking forward to getting to know more about him and his mission. Great bite size podcast and he DOES IT EVERYDAY!

★★★★★
Str8_Cash, 06/29/2018

The Best Podcast in The World
Dre set the bar for other podcasts around the world. Straight to the point, informative, honest, and an overall great platform.

★★★★★
BlueMan-NewMan, 06/15/2018

the path to prosperity
Thank you (and the team?) for what you do. You're changing lives for the better. I'd guess that you're getting enough feedback at this point that mine but I'm taking the time   more

★★★★★
bigmoose426, 06/07/2018

Life-changing
Dre's advice and insight will give you a whole new perspective on mindset and motivation. You will not regret taking 15-30 minutes of your time for this podcast.

★★★★★
Abdner, 05/16/2018

Not what I wanted to hear but what I need…
I've always struggled with being consistent and I finally decided that I needed some advice on what steps to take in order to be self disciplined and what not… I ended u   more

★★★★★
Spartacus in Vegas, 04/25/2018

The best
Definitely the most motivating and best content of any similar category pod cast. Keep it coming.

★★★★★
64writer, 04/20/2018

Always Working on my Fking Game**
I'm from Chester, PA and I probably spent some money with you at Footlock way back. Dre brings a starched clarity to self development. We should have more stra   more

★★★★★
David Hutcherson, 04/11/2018

Representation matters
So great to see a young black man doing his thing and showing others how to do the same in sports and business. Great job being an example for the African American comm   more

★★★★★
RemmiEllis, 03/02/2018

Would Pay For This
THE best podcast when it comes to progressing forward in life and being the person you need to be. Any obstacle or problem you have Dre has covered it in a   more

★★★★★
KayEssPee, 01/29/2018

Great Information
I started listening to this podcast over a year ago and I have been hooked ever since. Dre gives great advice that can be applied to every area of life. Great show!

★★★★★
Jrcivic, 01/22/2018

Great lessons
Man I wish I would've known about this podcast earlier. I was a talented soccer player in high school but never knew how to take losses or learn from my mistakes and ho   more

★★★★★
Mub33b, 12/21/2017

Phenomenal.
Love the podcast, as a fan of Dre from YouTube this podcast has been everything I expected & more.
The podcasts are concise and perfect   more

★★★★★
IAN DA BEAST5699, 11/28/2017

Top podcast for athletes but also for anyo…
I have been listening to leadership and motivational podcasts for years. I am an IT Manager and LOVE Dre all day!! I started listening for my young athletes - this is   more

★★★★★
tikNtie, 11/18/2017

Dre MOTIVATES me EVERYDAY
Thanks Dre!! You're the best.

★★★★★
Nama Soukouna, 11/16/2017

Great
Great podcast good way to start the day

★★★★★
GCGRoberts25, 11/07/2017

5 Stars !
Been watching for years now , love the podcast. Dre's quality and consistency is craaazy.

★★★★★
Daily YouTube Viewer., 11/06/2017

Highly Recommended
If you truly wish to improve your mental approach to life, listen to this podcast!

Work On Your Game Inc.
1300 Washington Ave #153
Miami Beach FL 33119

★★★★★
Combos Court, 10/13/2017

Good work
💪💪

★★★★★
Queenofhearts1979, 09/11/2017

Very effective
I love this podcast. I am upset I didn't discover it years ago. Dre is a great motivator who will go very far in his career because of his drive, philosophies, and direct approach to pro... more

★★★★★
Seanjezzy, 08/09/2017

Consistently amazing content
Dre will help elevate your game in every aspect of your life! I learn a lot from every podcast. Sustained excellence!

★★★★★
Daniel Trinks, 07/14/2017

Best personal development podcast
Every podcast I learn something new. Also I love listening to a podcast before my games and when I'm doing the dishes.

★☆☆☆☆
Shoffa79, 06/29/2017

No
Rambling

★★★★★
Eritrean-American guy, 06/19/2017

Speechless!
This podcast is literally "too good to be true", yet is is true! This entire podcast covers everything you need to hear in the world- especially for a basketball player! Dre ap... more

★★★★★
mjsatumba, 09/13/2017

🔑🔑🔑🔑🔑
Been following Dre for a minute, his YouTube videos have been inspiring and helpful in my life. Has been one of my best virtual mentors to date. Dre has been giving the 🔑🔑 more

★★★★★
April42479, 09/02/2017

Refreshing
Most dudes I know personally...like all...are so behind the ball in life. They are still subscribed to the blame game and pretty much living up to the low bar their neighborhood and p... more

★★★★★
dswimmer00, 07/24/2017

Great!
DreALLday is a beast! He gives good advice and motivates you to be your best! Would recommend!!

★★★★★
April *111979, 07/08/2017

Great podcast!
Great down to earth advice that I have found to be very helpful! Thanks Dre!!

★★★★★
Todd DeRouen, 06/23/2017

My Go-to Daily Podcast
I have two kids that are young athletes. Their attention span for my coaching is pretty short so I was looking for other "coaches" to get in their ears and heads. That's why I subsc... more

★★★★★
Wife of a snorer, 06/17/2017

Definitely a must!!!!!
His podcasts get directly to the root of the issue & gives crystal clear instructions for how to improve ANY situation or tackle ANY obstacle!!! His approach is extremely st... more

★★★★★
joshreese, 09/12/2017

Reminds me of best high school football c...
Dre cuts through and is ACTUALLY motivational. His passion is constantly on display.

★★★★★
cwb154, 09/02/2017

If You Haven't Started Listening to This Po...
This podcast will literally change the way you think. It will reprogram your brain and mindset to be completely bulletproof from any circumstance or challenge life throws a... more

★★★★★
Mr. and Mrs.X, 07/16/2017

Journey
I listened to the podcast and they were excellent. Full of valuable information and insight. My family and I will be purchasing some of his products. He has paid the p... more

★★★★★
ThisisVinsanity, 06/27/2017

Dre All Day is G.O.A.T.
He gives you amazing advice and I appreciate him.He gives you all about Mental Toughness, Confidence, and everything you have to know in life. This will help you benefit in life. T... more

★★★★★
Joog Season, 06/21/2017

1% better everyday
Dre been in his bag lately with these podcasts. @gijoey6

★★★★★
Bumbeen, 06/17/2017

Awesome
Excellent podcast

Work On Your Game Inc.
1300 Washington Ave #153
Miami Beach FL 33119

★★★★★
AF Hooper, 06/14/2017

Life changing
Dre is just continuing to flood our minds with positive and life changing ideas. Iv been a fan/student of Dre for about 5 years now and his podcast has become a daily must for me

★★★★★
Bryano58, 06/05/2017

Great Content
The content that is given on this podcast by Dre Baldwin are things you may or may not know, but the way Dre puts it out to his viewers can only be considered as a priv more

★★★★★
The NY Giant, 06/02/2017

Mandatory listening ™
Listening to this guy has been transformational in my personal development via confidence, self-awareness and accountability with my word. more

★★★★★
s.aubuchon, 06/01/2017

Highly recommended
Awesome resource for Personal & professional growth!!!

★★★★★
Justin Vanh, 05/28/2017

This podcast is 🔥🔥
I've been keeping up with Dre for a while now and he still continues to deliver value to the people. There are tons of episodes that you can find on almost any topic that you ca more

★★★★★
MarioMichaels, 05/27/2017

Work on your mental game
Dre has a lot of gems and there's nothing wrong with hearing old concepts with as many different angles as possible to internalize important information.

★★★★★
MiamiVice22, 05/27/2017

Inspiring and straight to the point!
I have been listening to Dre for almost a year now. His Podcasts are very easy to understand and filled with useful information. The information he shares on his Podca more

★★★★★
cjchambers17, 05/27/2017

Very truthful and real
You'll find very few people as honest as Dre Baldwin. If you want somebody to tell you straight up what you need to do to get where you want to be, he's your guy

★★★★★
DeeLane1906, 05/18/2017

Powerful Podcast
Dre has something that will reach you in his list of topics that give you power and confidence to be successful. I found it useful to help with starting my business and I c more

★★★★★
tdarden4life, 05/15/2017

I owe this man a check!
Listen, this guy is straight fire! The content value is unbelievable! I'm going to buy all of his books because I owe him money for listening to him each week and darn nea more

★★★★★
ArzuGosney, 05/15/2017

AMAZING!
I came across Dre's youtube videos when I was searching for answers for my daughter's Basketball game but he is much more than just basketball and now I am a huge fan! more

★★★★★
Hoselina, 05/11/2017

Words to Keep you UP UP UP
Treat yourself to this podcast and the tools he lays out to confront all of the challenges we face Day to Day.

★★★★★
Balling C, 04/24/2017

DreAllDay Helps my game
He just helps give people the mindset to become better at whatever they are doing! Great stuff and I don't like any other podcast.

★★★★★
MsMurphee, 04/06/2017

Great Podcast
Heard this guy on the DID podcast and loved his straightforward way of getting his message across! Many great lessons within one episode!

★★★★★
Nickname1221 波乗り歩, 04/05/2017

#WOYFG
💯💯💯 The best podcast in the world right now

★★★★★
DaniBertonatti, 04/05/2017

Extraordinary podcast!
I've been listening to Dre's podcast for a few weeks now and I can honestly say he's quickly become my favorite podcaster! Unlike many podcasts that interview other people an more

★★★★★
Zinobody, 03/28/2017

Best podcast out now
Listen to this everyday and it changes my life everyday I would recommend this to anyone who wants success and craves it

★★★★★
Michael Quartey, 03/28/2017

Mental energy
I listen to this podcast most mornings and every single episode has been relevant and helpful, I started watching dre all day videos on youtube years ago and these podca more

Work On Your Game Inc.
1300 Washington Ave #153
Miami Beach FL 33119

★★★★★
Dgblazer3, 03/21/2017
Dre is the GOAT
This man really knows his stuff. Everything he says is absolutely true and if it sounds harsh then you just gotta WOYFG 👍 A+

★★★★★
The hybrid Entrepreneur, 03/13/2017
Work On you Game
I highly recommend Dre's Podcast because the value of the content. Dre is inspiring me to start my own podcast one day. If self development is important to you, subsc... more

★★★★★
JBHATER420, 03/01/2017
Dre all day!!
I save nearly every episode that comes out on this podcast cause they're just so useful! Idk where my mind would be if I hadn't found this!

★★★★★
lisaann19104, 02/27/2017
highly recommend
excellent ideas presented quickly and concisely

★★★★★
Jelani Tonge, 02/26/2017
DRE ALL DAY
🤤🤤🤤🤤 HUNGRY 4 MORE ... Plan On Actually Meeting Dre Once My Success Comes . Get Ready To Receive Free Hoop Tickets To My Games When I'm In The A... more

★★★★★
Hyperswish, 02/26/2017
WOYG podcast
This podcast is great. It's the only one I listen too. Dre does help me. He gives me good ideas and tips. He lists out steps too. It's really helpful and can prepare me for life.

★★★★★
Sutaymc7, 02/19/2017
Nuggets
Dre offers a gold mine of knowledge that would be valuable to anyone regardless if you desire/are a professional athlete, business exec, teacher, preacher, doctor, undeci... more

★★★★★
Jean Leigh, 02/10/2017
Unexpected Podcast Mentor
I am the most unathletic tall person ever! So when everyone asks if I play basketball I laugh in their faces. And that's why it's so ironic that one of my best business mentors is a... more

★★★★★
AlexMoore23, 01/18/2017
Top podcast out today!
If you are looking to take that extra step in sports business or life overall then this is the podcast you need to listen to. Dre empowers you on a daily basis to succeed in life n... more

★★★★★
Tisani, 01/12/2017
New fan and doer
Inspiring, motivational and down-to-earth. Now I'm working on my own d@mn game!

★★★★★
Zacurry30russell, 01/03/2017
🏀🔑
Thanks for the vids and podcasts 👊

★★★★★
Tommy.Nguyen25, 01/02/2017
Life Changing
Dre helps you to stay locked in on your greatness with his teachings of discipline, dedication and hard work. A great mentor and someone who's always gonna keep it real.

★★★★★
Gpeter1540, 12/30/2016
Gets right to the good stuff
My favorite aspect about this podcast is that Dre gets right into what you want to hear. He never really goes off on a tangent and as a result, you get a podcast that is both ef... more

★★★★★
CLIPPERS FAN 32, 12/25/2016
Great
Love this podcast! Really made a difference in my life!

★★★★★
Saleskiller, 12/19/2016
The Real Deal
Tons of phenomal content and value.

★★★★★
iSebbb, 12/19/2016
Dre is the best
Everything I have ever asked for.

★★★★★
Madden Help, 12/19/2016
Advice On Everything
Dre has a knowledgable podcast on almost everything! His podcasts are very helpful and he always gives a nice summary at the end.

★★★★★
RayRay1510, 12/19/2016
Hidden gem
I originally found this podcast because I am an overseas hooper and related to Dre's story. However I have faithfully listened everyday since and am never disappointed. This... more

Work On Your Game Inc.
1300 Washington Ave #153
Miami Beach FL 33119

★★★★★
Fod's, 12/18/2016

SIMPLY GREAT!!
Keep up the good work Dre, this is great content for any players, coaches, parents, anyone that is trying to overachieve... Thank you for putting together and providing th more

★★★★★
MyMagnumDong, 12/18/2016

DRE IS THE BEST 🔥
To everybody looking at this you NEED to listen to this Podcast. Dre knows what he's talking about! #WOYG

★★★★★
Nba2 2 kyi, 12/17/2016

Great podcast
This gave me great advice on how to manage many aspects of my life and most importantly increase my confidence

★★★★★
856KiiNG, 11/26/2016

Great Information
Dre gives out great advice and life changing information.

★★★★★
Kevin Amison Jr, 11/21/2016

WOYG
The best podcast ever. Enough said. #WOYG

★★★★★
eddel_23(sauCeboiii), 11/16/2016

WOYG
I believe I'm the best and I'll always have that mindset

★★★★★
Anthony Kowalski, 11/16/2016

Best out there ! #WOYG
Nobody has ever helped me get a better understanding of anything, especially confidence or mental toughness than Dre Baldwin. Listen closely to every word, do more

★★★★★
Sreepoo, 11/16/2016

Amazing
Dre's podcast has taught me so many new things and helped me become so much more confident than ever before. Dre is simply the master at teaching you how to get that h more

★★★★★
SauCeboii from Snapchat, 11/15/2016

WOYG
Hesitation is a learned behavior...

★★★★★
YoungSinatra732, 11/15/2016

Great Work
Great work as usual Dre, keep it up!

★★★★★
Dannnnn😭😭😭, 11/15/2016

WOYFG!!
I been following dre from YouTube since 5 years ago, the man is a confidence genius and never fails to deliver insightful ways to approach new situations for entrepreneu more

★★★★★
Maestro Shabreon, 11/15/2016

Well Worth the Aural Real Estate
Dre gives you free access to the mindset of the ELITE.

You'll like the practicality of these episo more

★★★★★
iitz jemz, 11/14/2016

Great podcast
The man right here. Speaks nothing but facts

★★★★★
Sterling Inn, 11/13/2016

Excellent short podcast for achievement a...
Great episodes that are easy to listen to and digest.

★★★★★
javi_61797, 11/08/2016

WOYFG
I been following Dre Baldwin for years, starting with his youtube channel. I gotta say, this podcast is a MAJOR key to your success if you apply the concepts. Will definitely more

★★★★★
DavyboyPrime, 11/07/2016

Really great content
Dre covers basically everything you need to know to get up off of your butt and go make something of yourself. Don't pass up on this free knowledge.

★★★★★
IJR4, 11/06/2016

Phenomenal
Dre Baldwin has taught me so much on this podcast it is unbelievable. You can rest assured that you are getting high quality knowledge that you can apply to your lif more

★★★★★
JonesFromOAK, 11/05/2016

WOYFG Potna!!!
I listen to Dre multiple times a week. Pure gold. Also bought the mental handbook. Go get it, change ya life....!!! The WOYG podcast is on 1000.... Thx Dre!!!

Work On Your Game Inc.
1300 Washington Ave #153
Miami Beach FL 33119

★★★★★
Jcrossover0, 11/04/2016

Thank You!
Just wanna say thank you for creating this podcast. I listen to it every time I drive to and from work and it puts me in my "zone". Definitely worth looking into!

★★★★★
Insta: thejaydenmcadory, 11/03/2016

Every day
I listen to this podcast every single day. If you are in entrepreneurship, sports or you want to be a better person all around you should listen to this podcast.

★★★★★
amircd, 11/02/2016

Beneficial
Only reason why I use the podcast app. I have learned a lot from listening to this. I listen to it every night and every morning

★★★★★
kardos23, 10/31/2016

Must listen! 💯
Dre drops tremendous consistent value on this podcast. Anyone looking for personal development or motivation look no further! As a college student, I would have done any more

★★★★★
Kaizen Physical Therapy, 10/22/2016

Great Information for Everyone
Dre always delivers valuable information. I may not always agree with him, but I respect his point of view and learn from everything he says. Thanks for the value, Dre!

★★★★★
Mohamrygddgcdfgf, 10/22/2016

True inspiration!
Im jamal fahmi 22year old basketball player in Cairo, Egypt.
Dreallday podcast helps me with my game on the path of becoming a true professiona more

★★★★★
Kharon LaQua, 10/22/2016

DreAllDay
What can I say, I've learned so much from Dre. I like his personality, like his style, straight to the point, no fluff. He's real, raw, and tells it like it is. I look forward to Dre's post on more

★★★★★
ncschneid, 10/22/2016

Best hands down
Not sure how to be the person you know you should be? Listen. Pretty sure you know you're purpose? Listen anyway.

★★★★★
Patrick6142324, 10/21/2016

Major key!!!
Dre has more keys than dj khaled. This information is gold.

★★★★★
Ron Rucker, 10/21/2016

Work on Your Game
Powerful!!! Dre Baldwin is a Masterful teacher of the Mental Mindset and the Work on Your Game (WOYG) Podcast is a content driven, value added Blueprint to Success throu more

★★★★★
Ackempf, 10/20/2016

THE BEST PODCAST OUT
The WOYG podcast is by far the most beneficial podcast you can spend your time listening to. If you apply what you learn from here it can change your life for the bette more

★★★★★
Hfuydghfdfv, 10/20/2016

Dre is the best
Everyday you will become a better person because of Dres podcast

★★★★★
Jooossnsnjsssisisjsmsmsns, 10/20/2016

Shouldn't be Free, it's valuable
Dre talks about getting stuff done, and how to do the things you want to do. Listen everyday day cause DRE knows some valuable things most people forget or don't realize, tha more

★★★★★
nhydermvp, 10/19/2016

Dre Baldwin gives great advice
Podcast has a lot of great information that has helped me a lot with basketball.

★★★★★
Robertblount2, 10/19/2016

WOYFG
Been a fan for years. This man stays spitting knowledge

★★★★★
Zpzzzzzz1, 10/17/2016

Review
This is a great podcast, Dre is a really good dude and really sends a good strong message in these episodes.

★★★★★
The time is now 2016, 10/17/2016

Dre
A great podcast Dre tells it like it is. No "fluff". So much value. Subscribe to this now

★★★★★
SamuelHarrel, 10/17/2016

Motivating
I have been listening to the podcast for several months now. Dre consistently drops key after key, every single episode. I am a huge fan and would recommend this to more

Work On Your Game Inc.
1300 Washington Ave #153
Miami Beach FL 33119

★★★★★
leogarcia13, 10/16/2016

WOYG
Dre understands what it means to be successful. He understands what it takes. Really great podcast!!

★★★★★
Austin1500, 10/15/2016

DRE IS AMAZING
Some of the best motivational talks I've ever heard. Makes you want to literally "Work on your game" to be the best you possibly can be

★★★★★
Pierre G Koutani, 10/14/2016

GEMS
This is what you need to take to you to next level in anything, anything you need he probably has recorded on that subject. You will feel like he is talking directly to you more

★★★★★
Santos Samayoa, 10/14/2016

WOYG all day every day, Subscribe!!
Hey all, I first heard of Dre Baldwin on EOFire podcast, I soon found out he had his own podcast and have been an avid listener since. Dre drops words of wisdom, insight, and more

★★★★★
flowerbabyy, 10/14/2016

SO THANKFUL FOR YOU DRE!!
One of the best things that happened to me was coming across all of Dre's content! I make a habit of listening to him everyday! I can genuinely say his content has helped more

★★★★★
Lesballin, 10/06/2016

Dre Baldwin is simply the best!
Everyone needs to be listening to this all day!!

★★★★★
Darbinski, 10/05/2016

When in doubt Dre all day
I am so grateful to have stumbled upon this podcast! Dre is completely relatable and gives practical tools for living. He is well read and delivers his material in an honest but firm more

★★★★★
BB in WI, 09/27/2016

Bottom line- Dre helps me be better
He is a student of the game of life. His content is frequent. We all need daily seeds of positiveness. His style is also much better than others that are too much hype and more

★★★★★
MOE Student, 09/18/2016

MVH in MN
This guy dishes value everyday... totally inspires me to Work On My Game... no excuses!

★★★★★
1SamsonTheGreat, 09/03/2016

Golden Nuggets Galore
"Dre All Day". The nickname says it all. Dre provides a rapid and relentless onslaught of insight, truth, and motivation. Daily free breakfast of golden nuggets served fresh more

★★★★★
Cdub33366, 09/02/2016

Priceless information
First and foremost, I would like to say that this is one of the best podcasts on iTunes. The information that is given can be used in all aspects of life. This podcast focuses on more

★★★★★
BBHoap, 09/01/2016

The best source for mental toughness
Dre not only delivers a ton of value on mental toughness, but a lot of general life wisdom to boot

★★★★★
Craig-Winningyouthcoaching.com, 08/17/2016

Dre is an action taker and that is contagious
Appreciate this podcast, as Dre's passion and commitment flow through to inspire the audience to not make excuses and take action! Inspires me to keep on hustling.

★★★★★
DreBaldwin, 08/13/2016

Best Value in Podcasting
Dre has made a business out of delivering DAILY value - for your mindset, confidence, building your brand, and just plain motivation!
more

★★★★★
Manatiz, 08/10/2016

Sound advice, great tips
I listen to this podcast every morning and it helps me to improve my attitude and my outlook on success. I highly recommend this podcast for anyone who wants to succeed more

★★★★★
HarleyW2110, 08/02/2016

Constant flow of resource and information.
He can get you going if you need some motivation or make you work even harder than you already are. Great, knowledgable thoughts and information. I recommend more

★★★★★
Mike got the juice, 07/25/2016

DreAllDay
Been a fan and will forever be a fan. Great show. Great content. Always new and improving ideas .

★★★★★
Derek Nelson 819, 07/20/2016

awesome content!!
Dre, your show is for lack of a better word, awesome! I found you via EOFire and that interview was fantastic. Really looking forward to learning more from you. more

Work On Your Game Inc.
1300 Washington Ave #153
Miami Beach FL 33119

★★★★★
WonShotBA, 07/17/2016
Mamba Mentality
From one entreprenuer to another, hands down one of the best podcasts out there. Dre speaks in-depth about real-life applicable content and provides you with the exact more

★★★★★
Michael Gainer, 05/27/2016
The Best of the Best!!
This podcast will change your life! Dre will not only break down the content into simple terms but he gives you practical steps to take! It sprung me into action! And I'm already more

★★★★★
Actually the best on the Left, 05/06/2016
Awesome Podcast
I found Dre on Grant Candone Tv and I have to say this is propably the best podcast on how to improve my confidence & self-improvement I have ever heard. I'm not more

★★★★★
Cbh13, 04/27/2016
Great Info
Great information always responds to your email inquiries. Excellent motivational speaker

★★★★★
UnspOWken Assassin, 04/24/2016
The Realest !!!
I was listening today to one of his podcasts about "You Don't Have To Prove S*** To Anyone" and I though at that very moment he was a preacher but, I know in my life the more

★★★★★
Adubizzle50135, 04/21/2016
WYOG Pod
Great content that comes out daily. More young people need to shut their mouths and listen. A lot of opportunity and education that's free. Good work Dre.

★★★★★
Aeffrey, 04/20/2016
Dre has absolutely changed the way how I ...
Great man!!

★★★★★
44pastry, 04/19/2016
WOYG
Such a great motivational speaker. Hearing this guy talk habits, success, and routines is #1.

★★★★★
Fritzers164, 04/19/2016
Dre All Day is a must listen
Dre All Day is seriously the man. He knows his stuff. The content he covers on this work on your game podcasts is for all you entrepreneurs, business people, and ev more

★★★★★
Therealpinkmike, 04/19/2016
WOYG
Dre All Day!!! Enough said! Content! Quality! Truth! Knowledge! Real!

★★★★★
KingCarter52, 04/19/2016
Overall Podcast
The whole podcast is amazing, it has given me a huge amount of knowledge to help me In life now and help me to make smarter decisions in the future. He's definitely a more

★★★★★
zsn71, 04/12/2016
All Day
His nickname is Dre "All Day" for a reason; this is what he does day in and day out. Consistency is his strong suit and he's serving more out on here. His tips for productiv more

★★★★★
Burrnnout, 04/12/2016
To the Point. Effective.
Worthy of ur time

★★★★★
Hunt10/24, 04/12/2016
Dre is the man
I have learned more from him than any other person throughout the last few years.. He has positively influenced my life and without him paving the way for young entrepreneurs more

★★★★★
Anna Dolce, 04/11/2016
ABSOLUTE MUST!
Dre is a definition of WOYG. He lives and breathes everything he speaks about. Content he creates is an ABSOLUTE MUST read/listen to anyone seeking fresh and bold persp more

Work On Your Game Inc.
1300 Washington Ave #153
Miami Beach FL 33119

Jason Rivera

Happy birthday buddy.

The one thing you've shared with me that has helped me the most is that to succeed I need to believe in myself and what I'm doing.

And to do that I have to take the actions necessary to make things happen.

So all about building the confidence and belief in myself.

Has helped enormously.

Work On Your Game Inc.
1300 Washington Ave #153
Miami Beach FL 33119

Marilyn Nelson

Happy Birthday to you!
It only gets better from here!
Especially with a mind like yours.
My one thing is your consistent and consistently kind, solid, experienced, generous, and authentic message.
You are a giver who has fought your way through to the other side.
And through that came a quiet, sagely reserved, and giving nature.
Your generosity waters the beautiful flower you are and from here your garden will grow.
I hope you have an absolutely amazing 40th!
I am 50 and I sincerely mean it when I say life gets better, if you choose that:)
Happiest at all your birthdays!
Xoxox

Work On Your Game Inc.
1300 Washington Ave #153
Miami Beach FL 33119

Javier Fernandez

Today 10:35 AM

Happy Bday Dre! There's a lot you've helped me with. If I were to highlight one thing, I'd say the "third day" mentality. Sticking to the work even when the success you expected to achieve has yet to be achieved. Staying disciplined and focused on long term results over short term! Like Bruce Lee said, "I fear not the man who has practiced 10,000 kicks once, but I fear the man who has practiced one kick 10,000 times." 💯

> **David Eze**
>
> Today 10:41 AM
>
> Happy birthday Dre!
>
> You taught me how to change myself, so that I could change my life.
>
> My birthday is actually tomorrow so I'm glad to be a fellow Aquarius.
>
> I look forward to meeting you in person one day. You mean a lot to me.

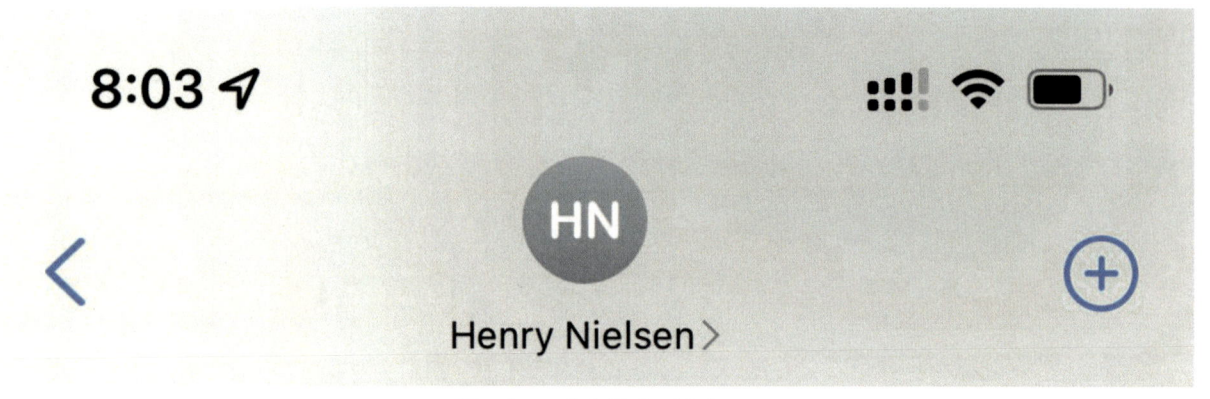

Work On Your Game Inc.
1300 Washington Ave #153
Miami Beach FL 33119

Henry Nielsen

Today 11:54 AM

> The ONE thing about you that inspires me the most is your consistency. I know exactly what to expect from you when I come to you for coaching.
>
> And you always deliver. No BS. Just the cold hard truth on how to get to the next level.
>
> Happy Birthday Dre 🏆
>
> #WOYFG

Work On Your Game Inc.
1300 Washington Ave #153
Miami Beach FL 33119

> **Evan Wallis**
>
> I'll give you three things
> 1. That how you talk to yourself and how you view yourself has a direct effect on how others view you
> 2. Only play in "games" where you have an unfair advantage
> 3. Life is a performance based business
>
> Ur the best Dre, happy birthday!

> **Strategic Intelligence:** Staying away from where you don't belong and focusing your time & energy on your strengths.
>
> Look where you want to go and not the obstacles in the way
>
> Be more thorough and detailed than your competition
>
> Receiving these daily messages have been such a for me I really appreciate you for who you are. Your willingness, ambition, and humility has been a huge encouragement for me and i know plenty of others. I have come a long way and i have to thank for that!!! Happy Birthday 🎉!!!!!!! Hoping you enjoy and this day is a blessing to you as much as you have been to others

— Julieh Clark

Angela Brickey

This is perhaps a general response rather than a specific point, but I would say your consistent, unapologetic ability to look at and articulate every issue from multiple angles. This has been particularly true as you have spoken on current issues. Your viewpoints have opened my eyes to see things in a new light, and in a sense given me "permission" (helped me be bolder) to ask more critical questions. I'm in a better position to push my students to do the same. I'm less likely to take the safe and easy route in terms of how I think about things and the positions I take, and therefore, I can set a better example for my students.

Work On Your Game Inc.
1300 Washington Ave #153
Miami Beach FL 33119

Who Do You Want To BE??? | Dre Baldwin

THE MAEZ PLAYGROUND · 1 day ago

Dre i been a fan since 2013 and u like a mentor to me i still watch your videos and teaching young kids fundementals i was 15 now im 27 and still working hard God bless

👍 6

Dre Baldwin - Work On Your Game · 0 second...

Good stuff my man appreciate you 💯

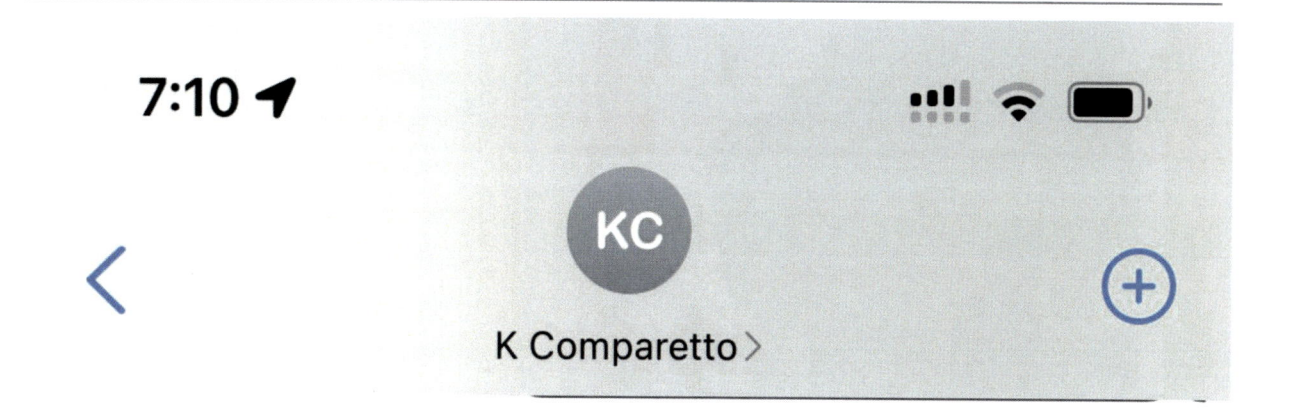

Work On Your Game Inc.
1300 Washington Ave #153
Miami Beach FL 33119

> **K Comparetto**
>
> Reading your third day book. 💪 thank you for everything you do. 🙏💙🙌

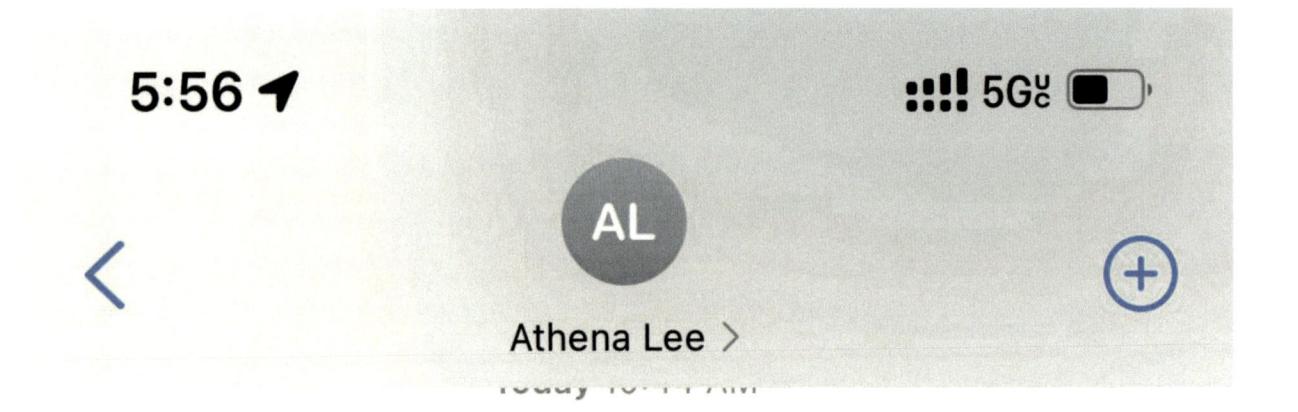

Work On Your Game Inc.
1300 Washington Ave #153
Miami Beach FL 33119

Athena Lee

> Emphasized "Everything and everyone will reveal itself in due time.
>
> #DailyMotivation #TheThirdDay"

> You just spoke exactly what is going on in my life right now. Wow

Work On Your Game Inc.
1300 Washington Ave #153
Miami Beach FL 33119

> Hello my name is Viggi love your videos bro just wanting to join the family please keep doing your uploads 💯💪

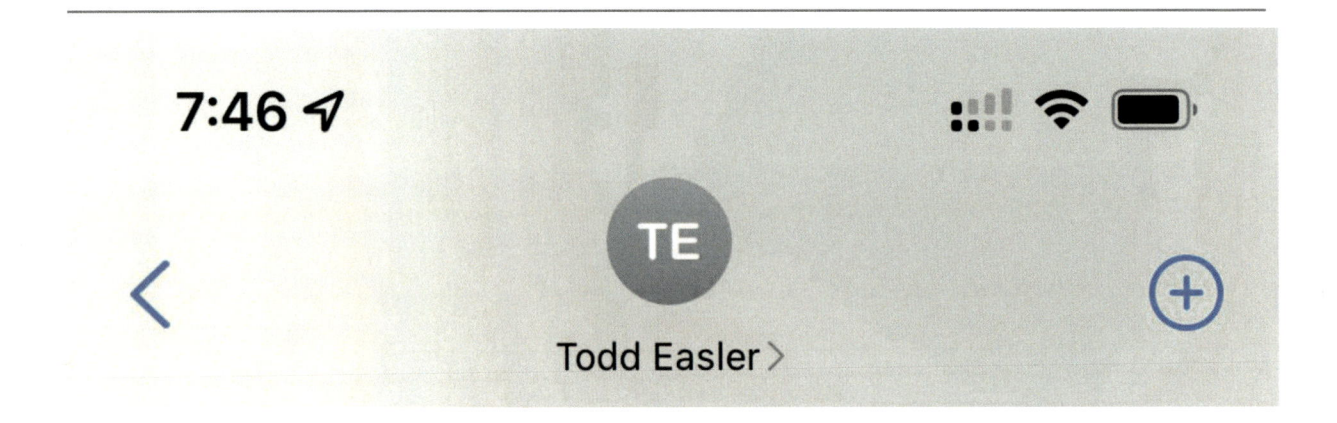

Work On Your Game Inc.
1300 Washington Ave #153
Miami Beach FL 33119

> Todd Easler
>
> Quote that immediately came to mind for today's podcast:
>
> If The Grass Is Greener On The Other Side, The Water Bill Is Higher !

Work On Your Game Inc.
1300 Washington Ave #153
Miami Beach FL 33119

> Thanks Dre, I just wanted to share that I was presented with the 2022 leadership award at my job. Your WOYG principals will always be instilled.

— Jim Jones

Rising Star Award Winner
Jimmy Jones III
Patient Care Associate
Waterbury Hospital

Work On Your Game Inc.
1300 Washington Ave #153
Miami Beach FL 33119

Selling Yourself | Dre Baldwin

Max Muscle & Fitness Athlete • 2 hours ago
Dre your daily text messages have instilled so much knowledge and action to my daily life professional and non professional life

👍 1

Max Muscle & Fitness Athlete • 2 hours ago
Shoutout to dre for helping me grow and mold myself into an outstanding person

👍 1

Work On Your Game Inc.
1300 Washington Ave #153
Miami Beach FL 33119

Durell Forte

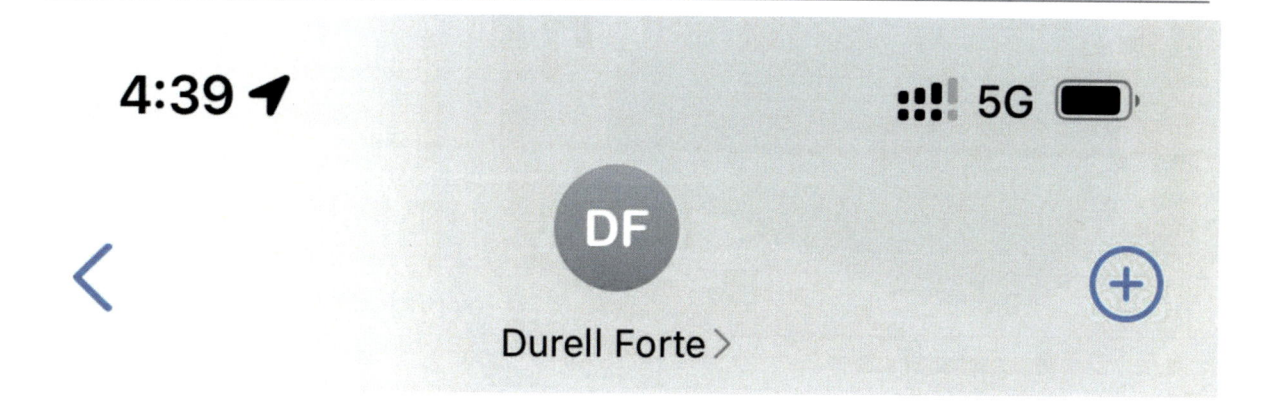

> Put my order in big bro trying to get back into my motivational speaking and your text have been helping and I know your books will give me everything I need

Product	Price
The Mirror Of Motivation [Book Only, USA Shipping] Access Member's Area Now	$9.95
Full Bulletproof Bundle [4 Books] Shipped Access Member's Area Now	$30
Leadership Bundle Upgrade [+3 Books, Free Shipping] Access Member's Area Now	$20

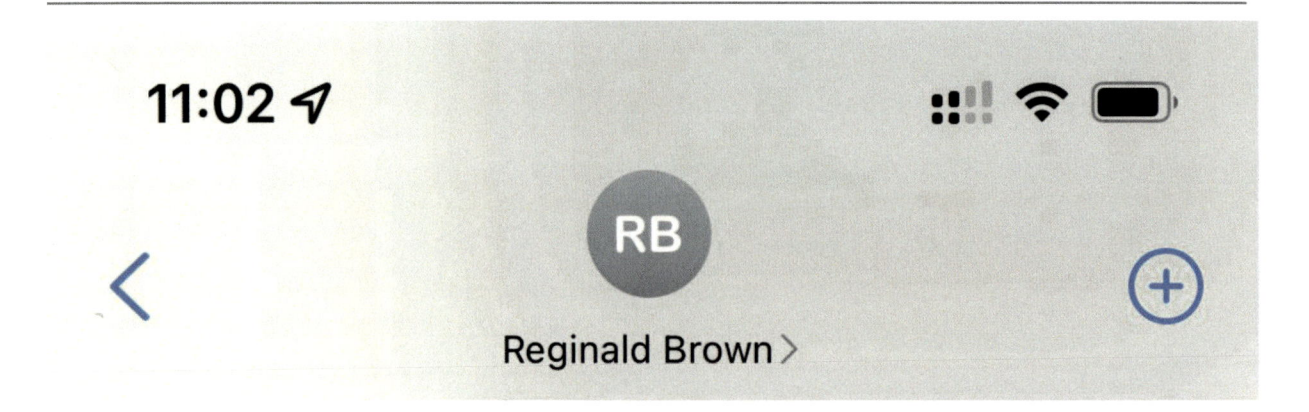

Work On Your Game Inc.
1300 Washington Ave #153
Miami Beach FL 33119

Reginald Brown

> Time is completely impartial to your circumstances. If you don't have time for something that's important to you, the only logical reason is in how you are managing your time.
>
> #DailyMotivation
> #TheThirdDay

Wow! Thanks for slapping me early this morning

Work On Your Game Inc.
1300 Washington Ave #153
Miami Beach FL 33119

Why Fear is Controlling You [#1813] | Dre Baldwin

brett patnode • 1 day ago

Man thus guy is incredible..! Just stumbled across this. You, sir, have a new subscriber

👍 1

Dre Baldwin - Work On You... • 0 seconds ago
💯 💯

4:44

Durell Forte

Just got mine in the mail yesterday

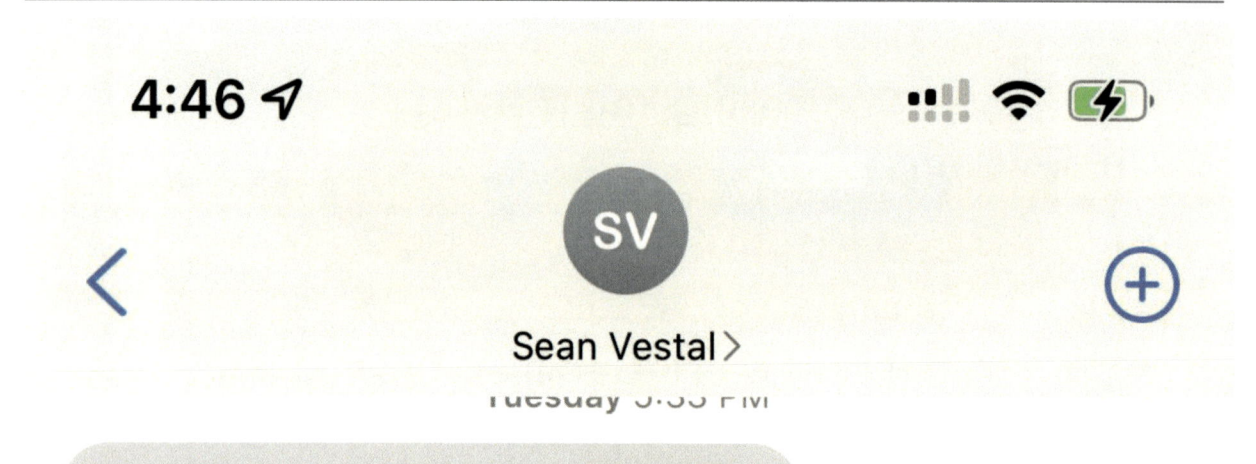

Work On Your Game Inc.
1300 Washington Ave #153
Miami Beach FL 33119

> Ep. 2185 is on point! SBDDD! Schedule Batch Delegate Delete and Defend! Masterclass on Time Mastery.
> — Sean Vestal

> I would like to be apart of the daily motivation community 💪

> Answer: I've been listening to your Podcast and YouTube since I was in the 8th Grade (7yrs ago) now I'm in the Army and received your number from your recent upload " Be The Smartest- Not The Loudest"... Big Fan of your Work and Legacy. Big impact to me; Thank you For everything! 💪✊

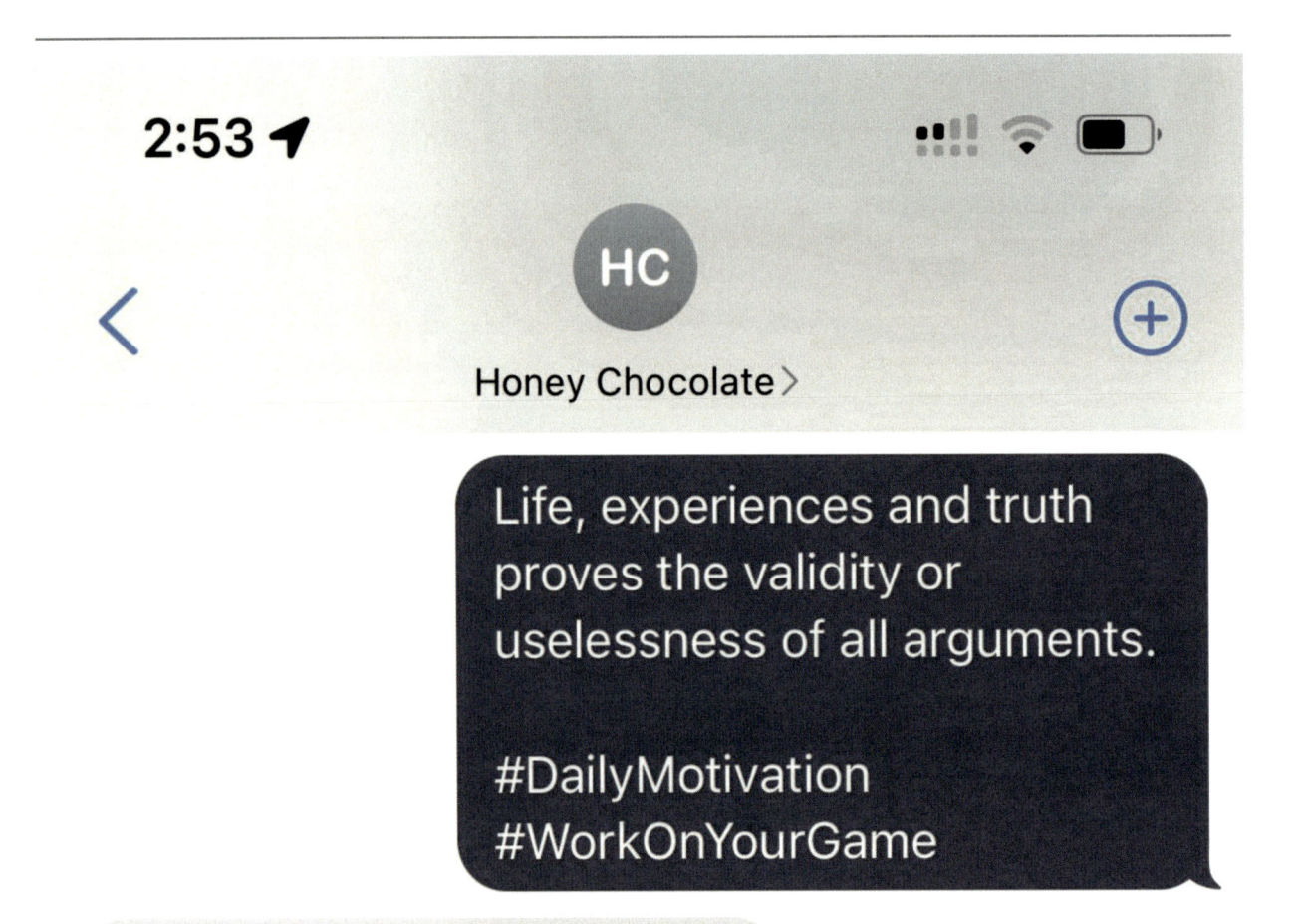

Work On Your Game Inc.
1300 Washington Ave #153
Miami Beach FL 33119

> Life, experiences and truth proves the validity or uselessness of all arguments.
>
> #DailyMotivation
> #WorkOnYourGame

These texts need to be on a 👕

Work On Your Game Inc.
1300 Washington Ave #153
Miami Beach FL 33119

Armani Comick

Hey Dre! I just saved you in my contacts. I love listening to podcasts, and I found yours on Apple podcasts browsing for some new shows similar to what I already listen to. Your show has blown everyone away, thank you so much

Raydgie Alexis

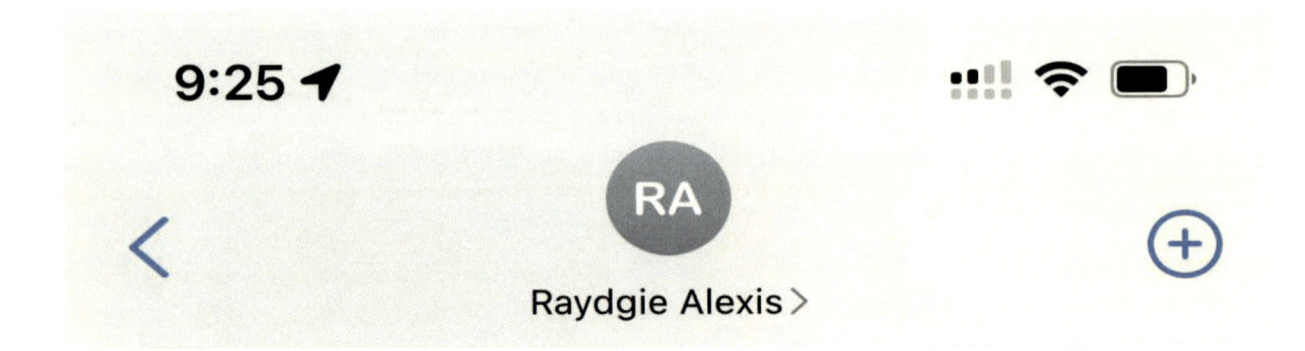

I came across your YouTube channel when told myself i needed to find someone that mixes sport and mindset as a coach, after some research, movies, algorithms and I lil bit of luck I found my answers through a video you've made that no one was talking about. For that I thank you.

Then I tried to binge watch and discovered the amount of content lol and then I got to your other plateformes and still today I am shook.

It's been 2 months, I've been improving good & assisted your last event and now with your daily motivation texts.

Javier Fernandez

Dre, the email you sent this morning was such facts! Love the Shake Shack & sports car analogies 🔥

"Average people make choices that will benefit them NOW. Exceptional people make choices that may not be so fun NOW, but will be 10X more satisfying in the future than the pleasure the masses get for their NOW decisions today."

"The exceptional few who exercise a strong time perspective aren't necessarily smarter or luckier or harder-working than those who habitually seek instant gratification.
They just have a simple discipline, executed consistently, that doesn't make much impact in the moment, but accumulates into a huge

Work On Your Game Inc.
1300 Washington Ave #153
Miami Beach FL 33119

Armani Comick

Yesterday 11:01 PM

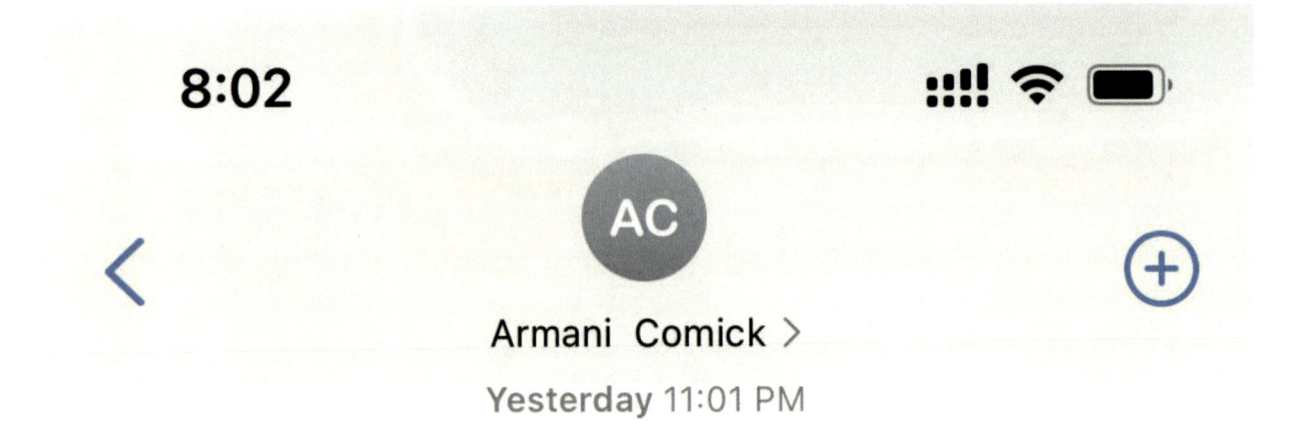

> Just finished listening to these two episodes. They both had things in it that I needed to hear. I've never even once considered what I can eliminate. I usually spend this time after work sitting scrolling and trying to decompress. Taking in news and focusing on others peoples business is not a productive use of my time. Today, I listened to these episodes and learned a lot. I scheduled a 1:1 call with you. Looking forward to speaking about this more

> Some great points and ways to approach and attack life I've learned from you just watched another video today 👍 +1

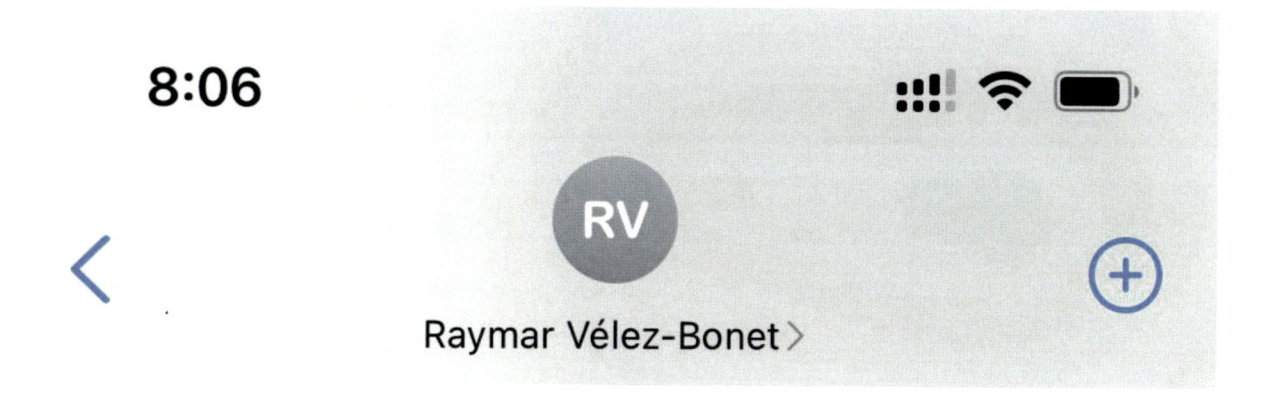

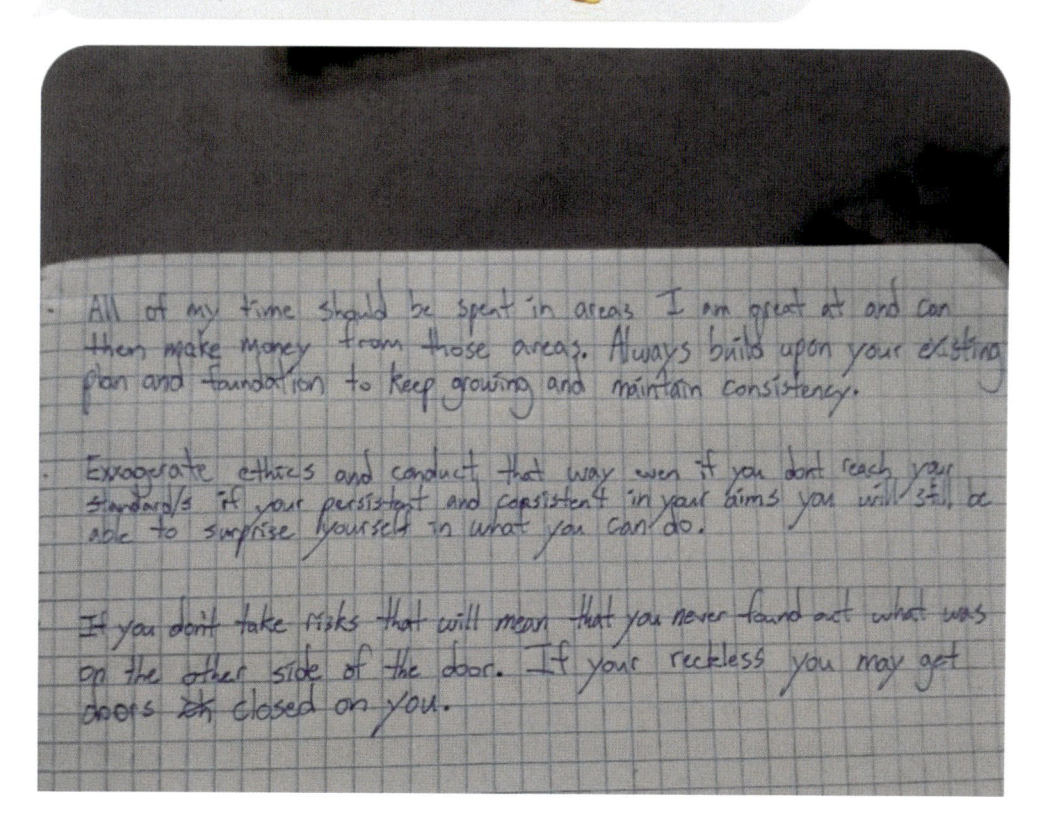

- All of my time should be spent in areas I am great at and can then make money from those areas. Always build upon your existing plan and foundation to keep growing and maintain consistency.

- Exaggerate ethics and conduct that way even if you don't reach your standard/s if your persistent and consistent in your aims you will still be able to surprise yourself in what you can do.

- If you don't take risks that will mean that you never found out what was on the other side of the door. If your reckless you may get doors closed on you.

Work On Your Game Inc.
1300 Washington Ave #153
Miami Beach FL 33119

Reagan Brown

🙂

Yesterday 9:00 PM

I was looking for a podcast to help me with my mental toughness and as an athlete your podcast title stuck out to me.

Work On Your Game Inc.
1300 Washington Ave #153
Miami Beach FL 33119

> I'm starting to realize if I don't take notes I'll lose most of the valuable information you gave me. I just wanna give you your flowers man your really my life coach and we ain't even meet yet. Keep being great 💯
> Woyfg 4L

Denise R. Russo

Fascinated by Leadership Development and Human Behavior, Success Coaching, Writing, and Ikigai

WEDNESDAY

Denise R. Russo · 10:53 am

Thanks for accepting the invite. Your session at ATD was awesome, relevant, easy to understand, and more. It should have been a sold out room. Thanks for all you do.

Ebony Hood

> Thanks Dre!

> Hey Dre, I've been following you for years & just wanna say Thank You for always making yourself available to players/coaches like me. I appreciate you and the knowledge you share. ✌🏾😊

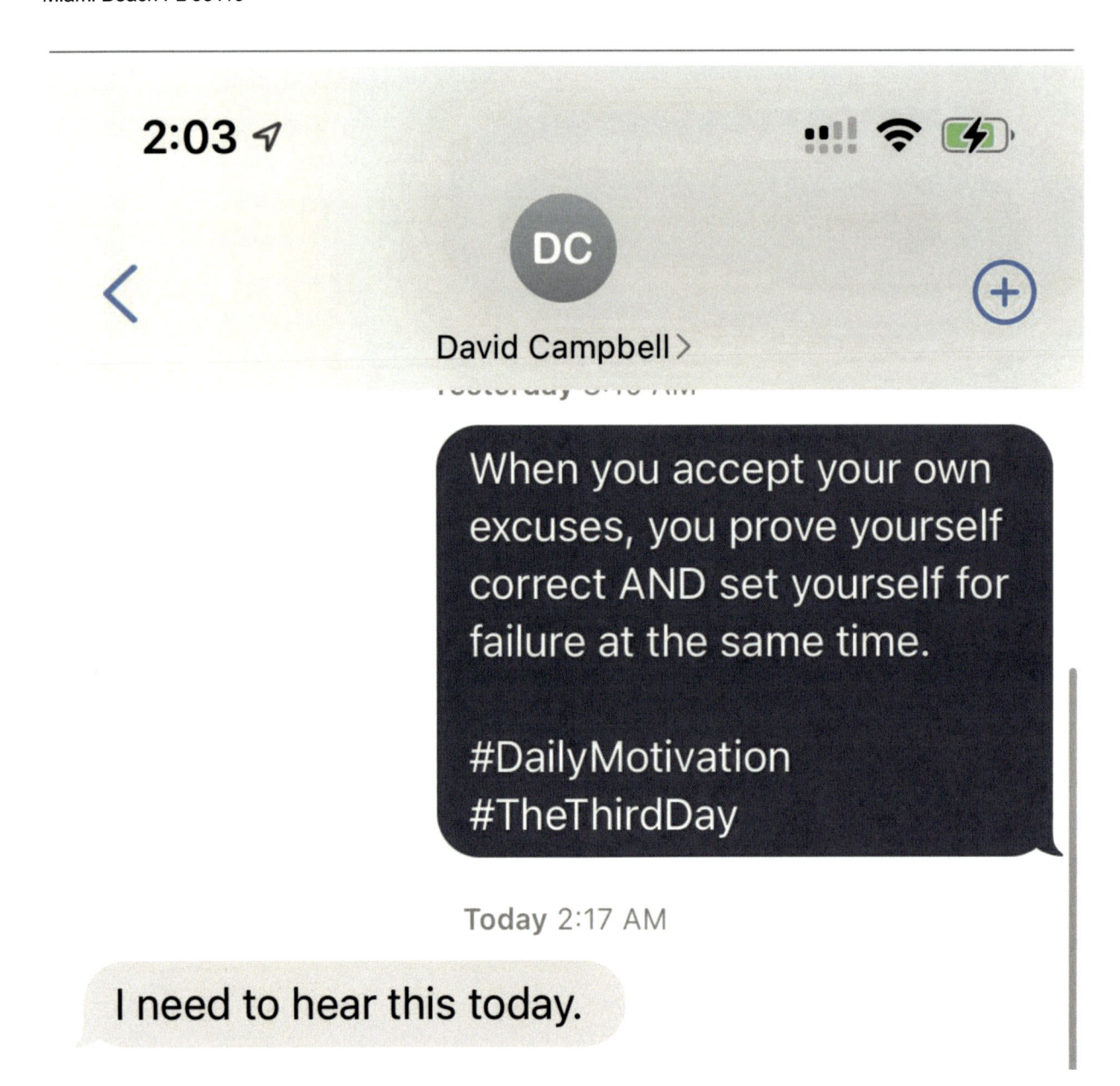

Work On Your Game Inc.
1300 Washington Ave #153
Miami Beach FL 33119

David Campbell

> When you accept your own excuses, you prove yourself correct AND set yourself for failure at the same time.
>
> #DailyMotivation
> #TheThirdDay

Today 2:17 AM

I need to hear this today.

Work On Your Game Inc.
1300 Washington Ave #153
Miami Beach FL 33119

> Loved "People are more often held back by poor mental habits than by poor strategy.
>
> #DailyMotivation
> #TheThirdDay"

> Hey Dre, just wanted to say that I think work on your game is truly the best mental toughness and discipline method/ philosophy/ class and you've helped me overcome a lot of extremely difficult times in my life and I'm very grateful for everything I've learned from you.

> **COLIN BAGLEY:** Just got the 3rd day book ordered. Looking forward to it!

Nicholas Flack

What's up Dre, I just watched episode 1914 and it has benefited me immensely. I specifically related to the part you said about it being your responsibility to get yourself out of bad situations. Thank you dre, your life advice is very appreciated. I'm not sure if you have made a episode about speaking and sounding more educated and intelligent, but I think it would be great. Thanks Dre!

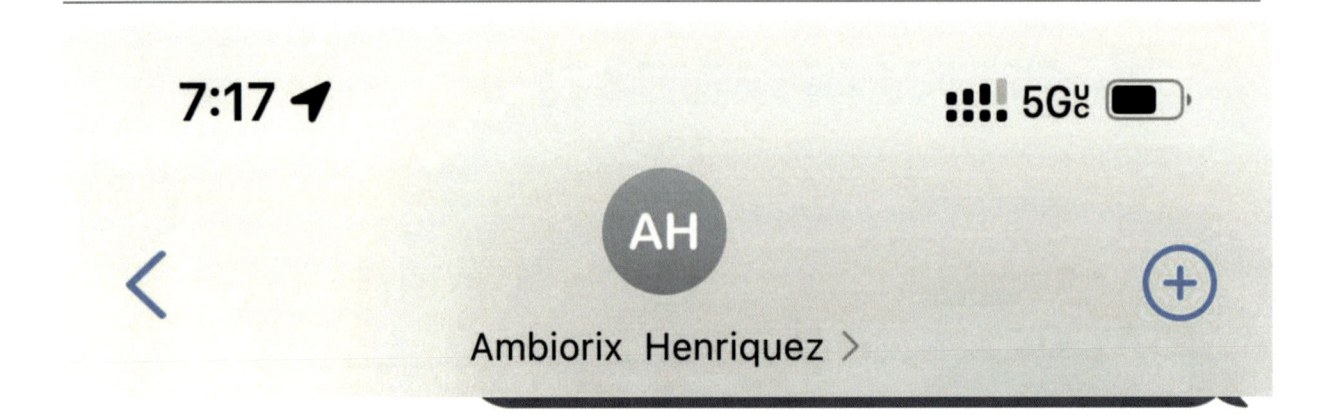

Work On Your Game Inc.
1300 Washington Ave #153
Miami Beach FL 33119

Ambiorix Henriquez

> Just letting you know I been watching your videos since 14 years hold! I'm 20 right now

> And I'm currently doing real estate! And number one challenge is making my own decision and taking control on what I want to do

Work On Your Game Inc.
1300 Washington Ave #153
Miami Beach FL 33119

Jordan Cicchesi

> Hi Dre thank You your books are Uplifting and Life changing

Work On Your Game Inc.
1300 Washington Ave #153
Miami Beach FL 33119

Saksham Ghai

> I'd love to work with you. I'm not sure how much this costs but I'm building up my Real Estate Agent business and in my early stages so I don't have lots of money right now. Will become financially successful and join your coaching. 👍

> Sounds good. The way it works is the other way around — coaching is how you become successful. Join the Mastermind if not the 1x1

Work On Your Game Inc.
1300 Washington Ave #153
Miami Beach FL 33119

Xavier Johnson

Thank you! I'm from Dallas, TX. I been listening to your podcast & YouTube videos since I was 14 playing basketball . I'm 22 now & I'm a growing entrepreneur. I've also listened to a few of your audio books! I recently needed inspiration again & after maybe 2 years went back to my "roots" and realized you definitely helped me develop a strong business mindset growing up. First through the love of basketball, then my favorite entrepreneurship! @deepwave_x on Instagram 💯

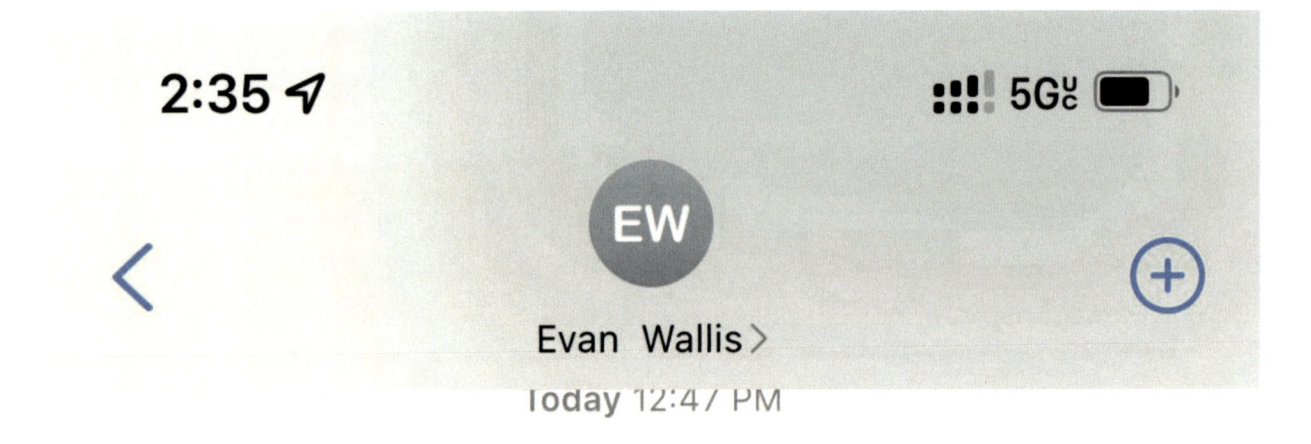

Work On Your Game Inc.
1300 Washington Ave #153
Miami Beach FL 33119

Evan Wallis

Today 12:47 PM

Wow that's really helpful, I appreciate you taking the time to link them, thanks dre!

It's pretty incredible how I'm actually talking to you...like I've been watching and listening to you since I was 13 and now I'm texting you 😹 surreal

Today 2:35 PM

💯 The internet is incredible

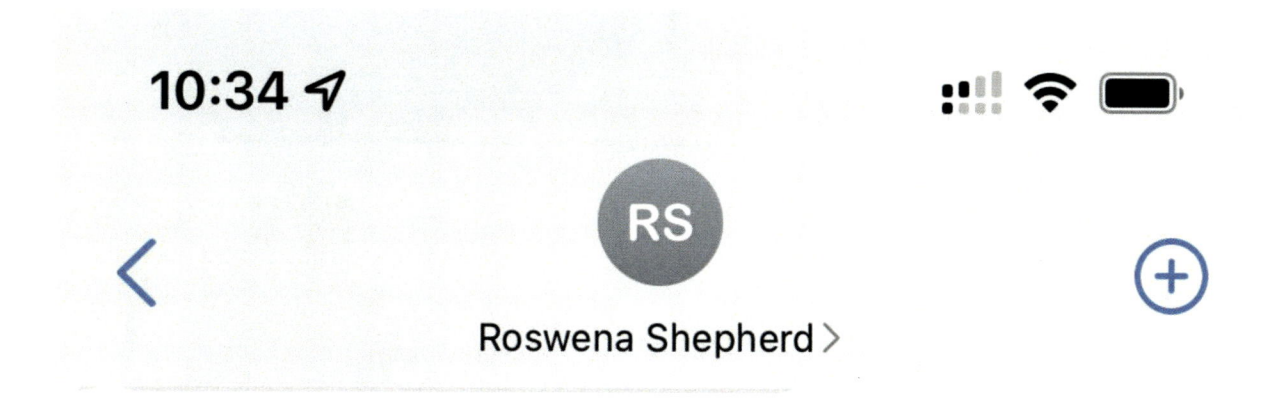

Work On Your Game Inc.
1300 Washington Ave #153
Miami Beach FL 33119

> Great morning, I just wanted to say I love your Daily Motivation and thank you it is very much appreciated.
>
> Have a great and amazing day!

— Roswena Shepherd

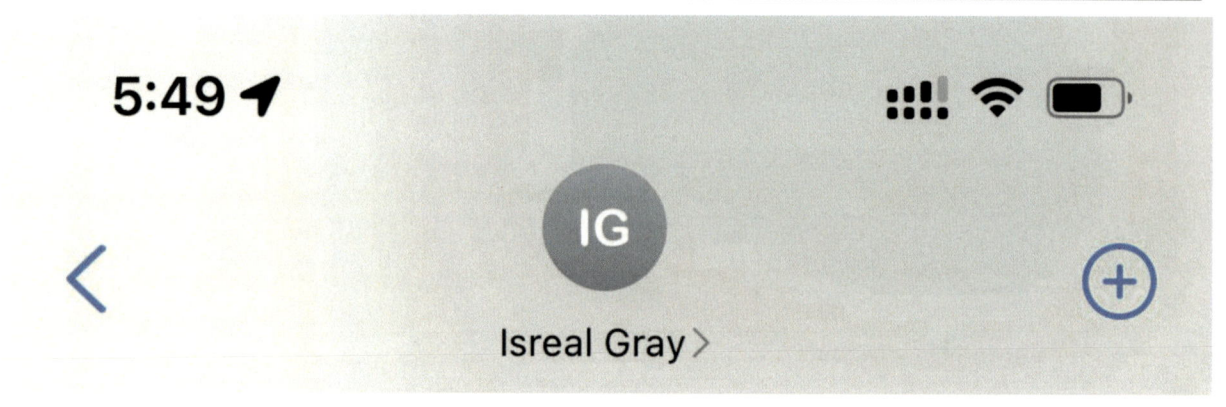

Work On Your Game Inc.
1300 Washington Ave #153
Miami Beach FL 33119

Isreal Gray

Today 9:36 AM

> I really appreciate all the work you've been putting in, thank you!

Today 5:49 PM

Thames Bennett

> Dre, I got the job! No more Under Armour. Thanks for the daily motivation 💯

Work On Your Game Inc.
1300 Washington Ave #153
Miami Beach FL 33119

Tammy Harper

💯💯💯 Good morning Dre! I am 1/3 through The Third Day! A POWERFUL concept that confirms why I am successful! Also I am the A&R to an artist who performed on the taping of The Stellar Awards on Saturday night...she was AMAZING! Got lots of accolades from my CEO that I did a "Stellar" job with all the details leading up to her performance yay! This is me at the after party! Have a great day! ☀️

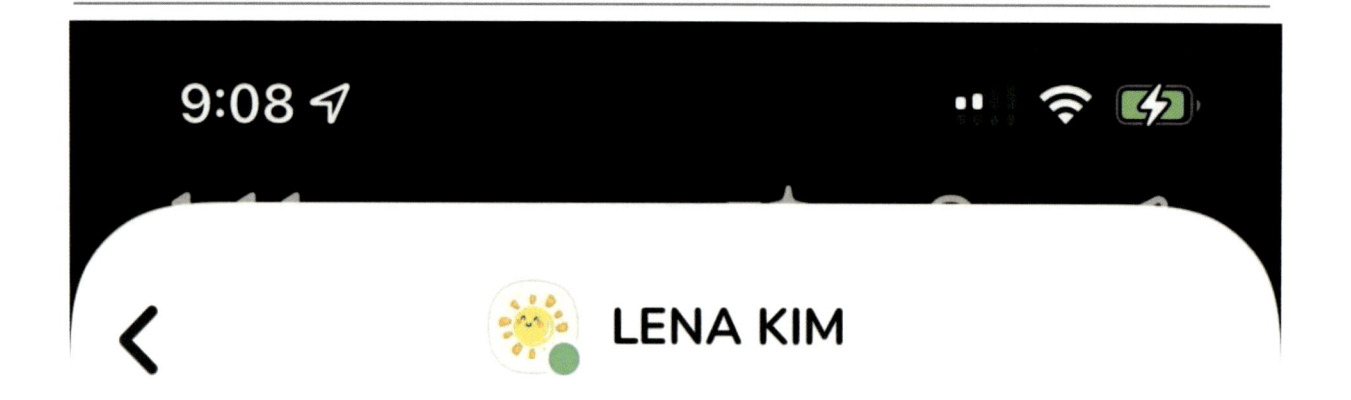

Work On Your Game Inc.
1300 Washington Ave #153
Miami Beach FL 33119

LENA KIM

Today 8:45 AM

Big lessons 💖💖💖
Ahhhmazing and inspiring speech !
Thank you 😊😊😊💚💙💚💕

I will soon re-listen to it and take a note. Wow. 🥹

Work On Your Game Inc.
1300 Washington Ave #153
Miami Beach FL 33119

JESSICA M. POWERS

Today 10:40 AM

"When you alleviate yourself of responsibility, you alleviate yourself of your power too. They go hand in hand." - Dre Baldwin 🔑🦁🔥

Powerful insight, Dre

8:40

Messages   **Marico Thomas**

that youtube video you dropped today was everything like always brother 💪💪💪

Work On Your Game Inc.
1300 Washington Ave #153
Miami Beach FL 33119

BOBBY JOHNSON

Sunday 9:08 AM

Dre All Day!!! Man I'm 19 and I swear everyday you get me where I need to be in a bold and authentic way!

10:09

Messages **Charde Moore**

With these questions... you made me change my mind. My biggest issue is discipline, not obscurity. Thank you so much for helping that realization! 🙏

Work On Your Game Inc.
1300 Washington Ave #153
Miami Beach FL 33119

mr michigan

⭐⭐⭐⭐⭐ **Awesome book! Dre Baldwin does it agin.**

Reviewed in the United States on December 26, 2014

Verified Purchase

Another great book from dre. I loved his 'buy a game' book, which is also a must read. In this book dre digs deep and gives out so many nuggets of wisdom that will help you get motivated and on track if you have been slacking, which I have.

In the book dre goes over how our negative thoughts keep us from accomplishing our goals and how we need to adopt a 'winning mindset'. He doesn't just speak about sports but all faucets of life and work. If you want to get motivated and become something bigger than you are right now, then the advice in this book can help you get there.

Keep doing your thing dre.

Henry Nielsen

⭐⭐⭐⭐⭐ **Fantastic Book!**

Reviewed in the United States on January 30, 2017

Verified Purchase

Dre Baldwin never fails to deliver top notch quality in anything he puts his name on. If you're looking for motivation or to be motivated, this book will not only do just that. It will teach you how to find motivation in yourself, not in other material things outside of yourself that wear off after a few days. Anytime you begin doubting yourself or wondering why you are doing what you're doing, the most profound and groundbreaking motivation that you'll ever find is when you look at yourself in the mirror and see how far you have come and tell yourself how far you want to go. I recommend this book for everyone of all ages, genders, nationalities, etc... for everyone and anyone!

Work On Your Game Inc.
1300 Washington Ave #153
Miami Beach FL 33119

N. Johansen **VINE VOICE**

⭐⭐⭐⭐⭐ **Invaluable.**

Reviewed in the United States on October 5, 2013
Verified Purchase

I'm not sure how I stumbled across Dre Baldwin's YouTube videos; I don't play ball, and I have little desire to improve my crossover. Aside from the basketball tips 'n tricks, he posts a motivational video every week, with a bit of wisdom from books he's read and his lengthy, winding path as a pro baller. THE MIRROR OF MOTIVATION takes many of these ideas, along with some new ones, and places them in written form.

And Dre is spot-on.

In short, these are not platitudes of someone who is trying to craft a frivolous best-selling self-help book. These are principles he lives by. You can hear it in his voice, see it in his work ethic, feel it in the way he plays ball. This is a man dedicated to his craft, who has put in countless hours of hard work. He knows how to get it done, and he lays it all out in simple terms. He doesn't mince words, and he doesn't fill this book with feel-good nonsense. It's direct, to the point, and, unlike most motivational books, actually applicable.

Why? Because it doesn't come from an author hastily slapping words on the page in nice sounding, empty sentences. These ideas are born of dedication to his craft. They are the thoughts of a professional, the product of many, many years of effort. As such, they are invaluable, particularly to those who are at the start of their journey towards mastery and greatness. To anyone interested in these things -- in any area of life -- THE MIRROR OF MOTIVATION is an excellent, quick read. It's not without problems; it could use a proofreader, and the formatting is a little wonky in a few places. These don't detract from the information; I just believe it could have used an extra layer of polish.

Small quibbles aside, this is a book well worth picking up; it'll save you a lot of time and money searching for "secrets" and other quick shortcuts. There aren't any, as Dre mentions numerous times -- the only way to improve, in whatever your craft may be, is to, as he says at the end of every video, "work on your game."

Giasparadise

⭐⭐⭐⭐⭐ **The Mirror of Motivation is truly inspiring.**

Reviewed in the United States on November 27, 2015
Verified Purchase

A very Motivational and truly inspiring book. The mirror of motivation is a book everyone should read. In Dre Baldwin motivational book helps you realize you can turn your pain into motivation. Gives you the motivation to Make plans bigger than yourself. This book was uplifting and very motivating. I definitely recommend this book.

Work On Your Game Inc.
1300 Washington Ave #153
Miami Beach FL 33119

Amazon Customer

⭐⭐⭐⭐⭐ **I love this book because you learn everything you need to …**

Reviewed in the United States on August 6, 2016

Verified Purchase

I love this book because you learn everything you need to know in life to make sure you're successful. I personally think this book is even better than the Mental Handbook. This one is longer and it focuses on what you need to do in order to get the best out of life. There were a few errors but not much like the Mental Handbook!

Blake and David❤️

⭐⭐⭐⭐⭐ **No lies detected**

Reviewed in the United States on August 3, 2021

Dre is always on point, doesn't miss when it comes to his philosophy, I've bought 4 of his books and they're some of the best investments I've ever made. If you want to take your game to the next level this dude is definitely for you. I'd give 100 stars if I could

Robbie

⭐⭐⭐⭐⭐ **10/10 Great Book**

Reviewed in the United States on July 20, 2021

I've never been someone who leaves reviews, but I had to on this book. I've followed the author, Dre Baldwin, for a number of years. Everything he puts out is gold, but this one is on another level. It's given me a new mindset and mentality to tackle my goals & stop procrastinating. It's helped me build personal discipline in all areas of my life, beyond work and athletics.

I seriously never write reviews like this. I wouldn't be recommending this book if I didn't buy it myself & enjoy it.

Work On Your Game Inc.
1300 Washington Ave #153
Miami Beach FL 33119

MikeSizz
⭐⭐⭐⭐⭐ **A how to book of sorts to become a better version of you**
Reviewed in the United States on February 22, 2019

Admittedly I was scared of success. Although I still feel that way from time to time it has never hindered me as it has before.
I still haven't reached my goal of playing basketball at the highest level BUT this was the book I read leading up to my first professional (ABA) tryout. Whether the confidence I gained in myself was because of the book or the sheer amount of work I put in just prior, we'll never know.

However, the result was I was done being afraid of who the best me was and could be; I was now not just me, but The Super Me.
Lo and behold I made the team.

Not saying you'll have results as such, you are after all going to need to 'Work on your game' however what I am saying is that it's very possible to change your belief in yourself and start doing things you were previously dreaming of doing.

Take a chance and read this book. You won't regret it

ANON
⭐⭐⭐⭐⭐ **Gains of CONFIDENCE**
Reviewed in the United States on November 5, 2016

In "The Super You" Dre Baldwin details how to get that super you (the you you want to become but afraid being). It's very detailed and has personal experiences people like you can relate to. We all have our moments struggling with confidence and that is where practicing our mental games comes in. Baldwin also provides very detailed and applicable mental game practices which in result boosts your confidence to where you would like it to be. I recommend this book greatly as it did boost my mental game up.

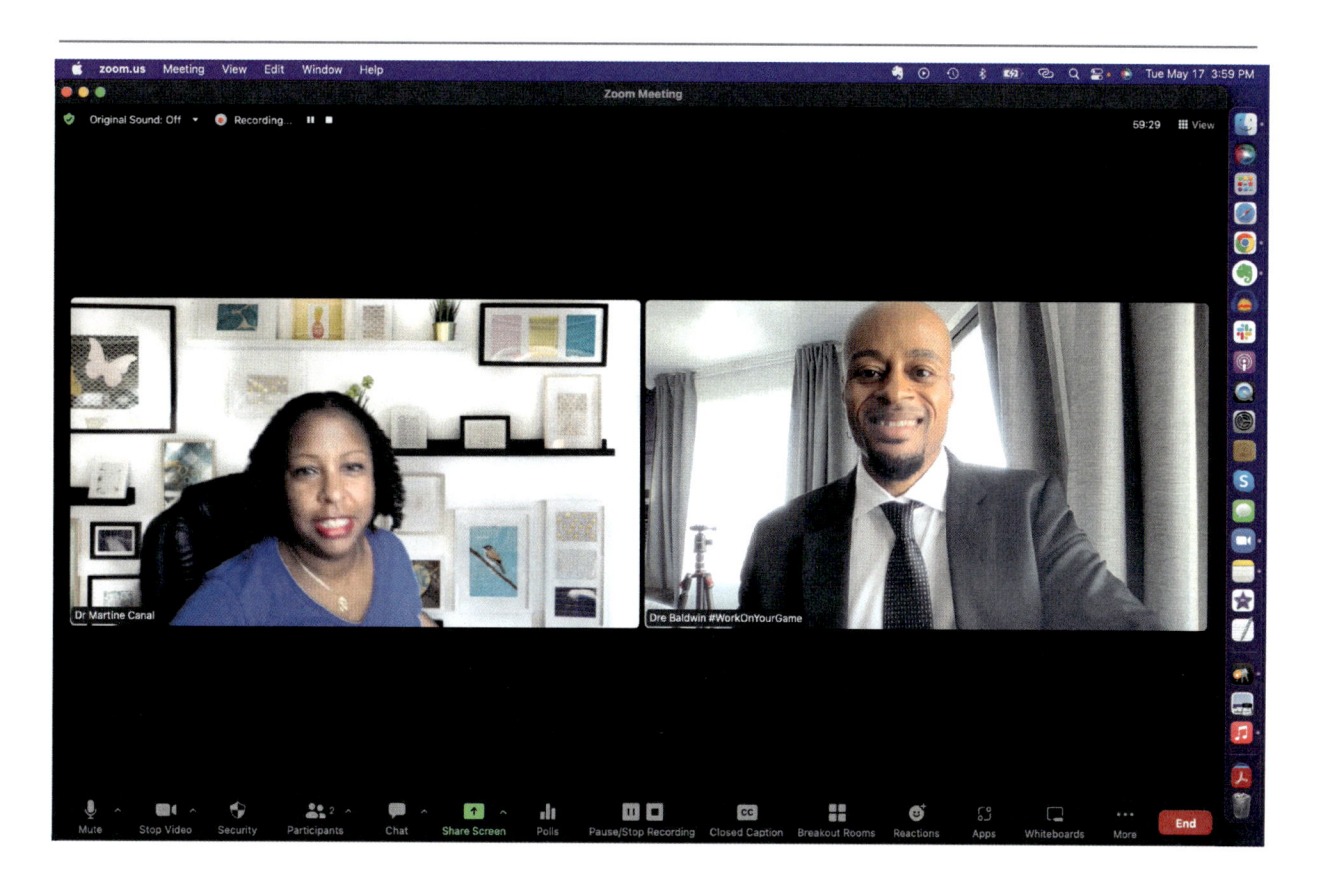

Work On Your Game Inc.
1300 Washington Ave #153
Miami Beach FL 33119

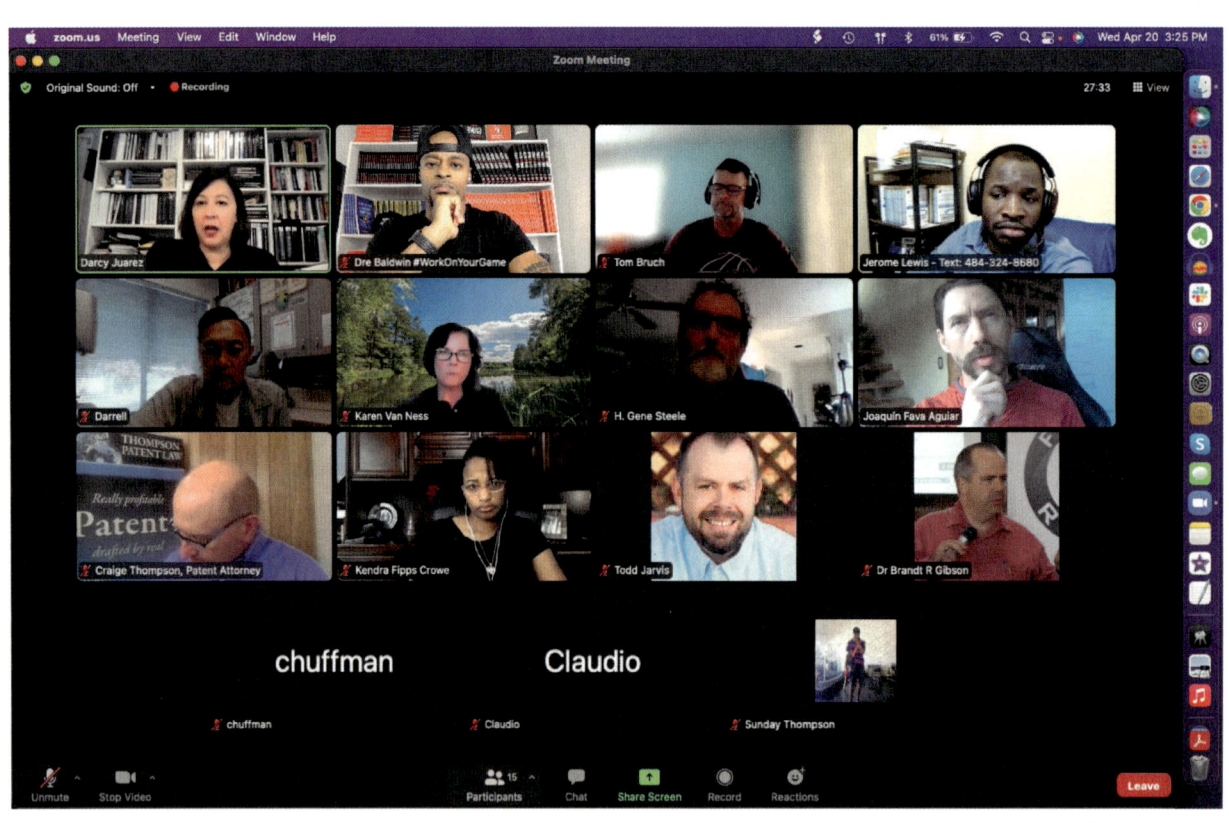

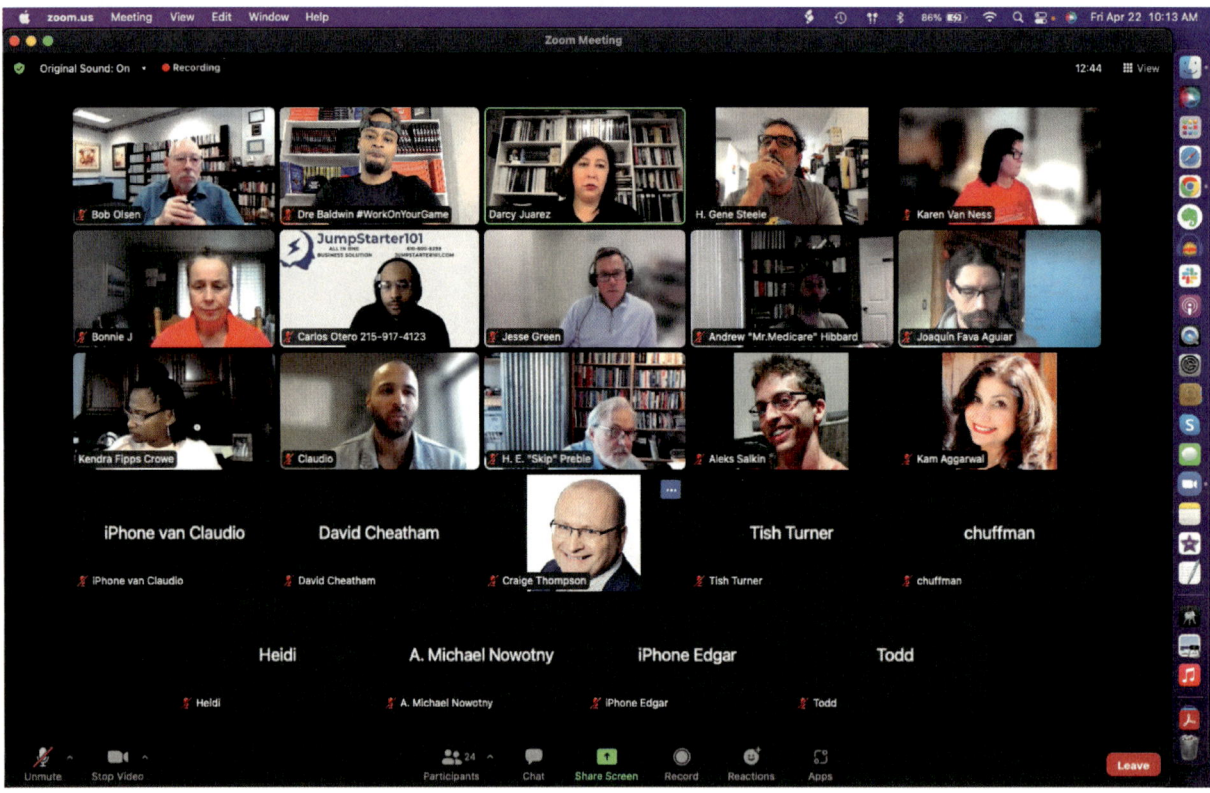

Work On Your Game Inc.
1300 Washington Ave #153
Miami Beach FL 33119

Work On Your Game Inc.
1300 Washington Ave #153
Miami Beach FL 33119

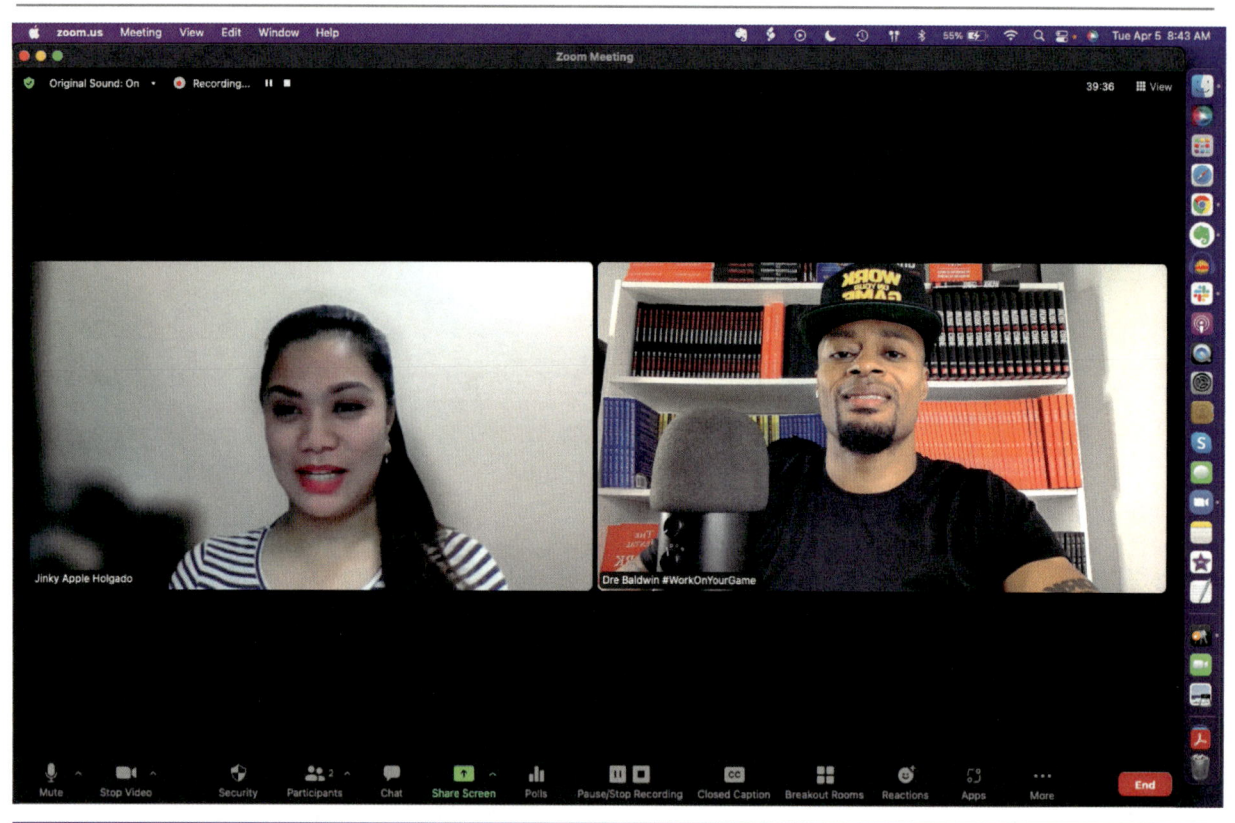

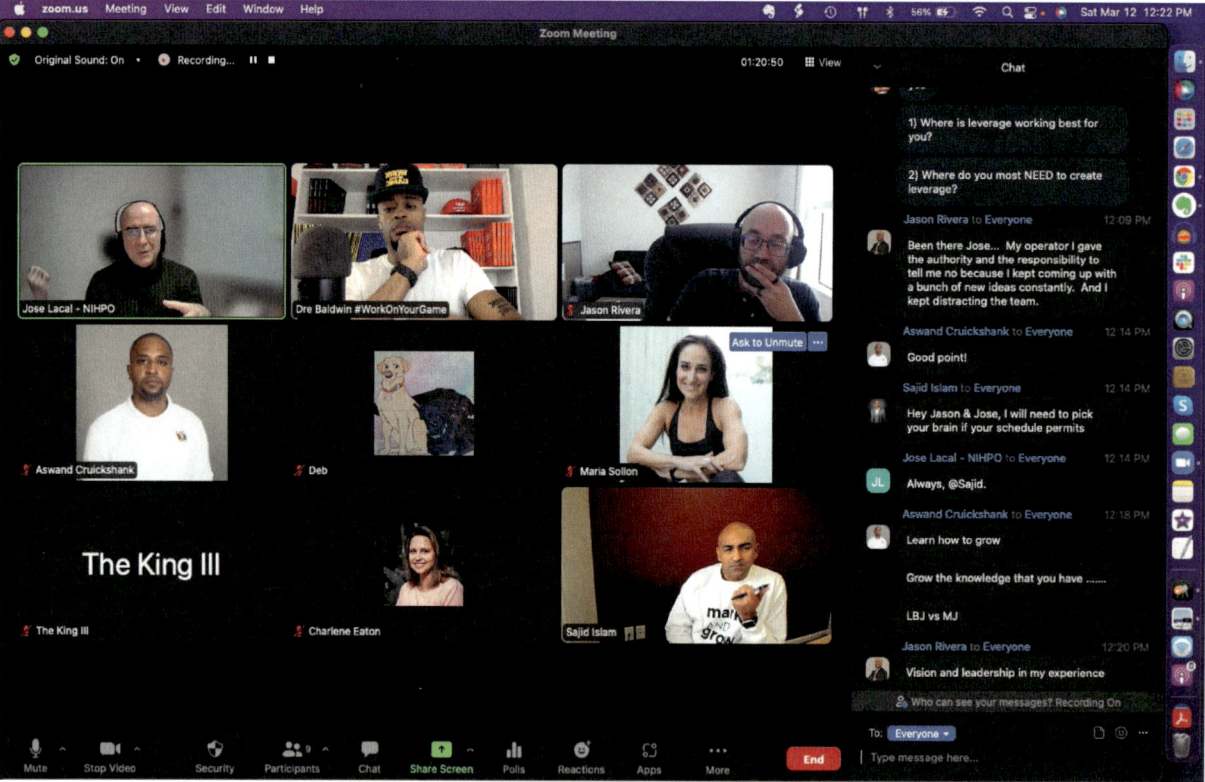

Work On Your Game Inc.
1300 Washington Ave #153
Miami Beach FL 33119

Work On Your Game Inc.
1300 Washington Ave #153
Miami Beach FL 33119

Work On Your Game Inc.
1300 Washington Ave #153
Miami Beach FL 33119

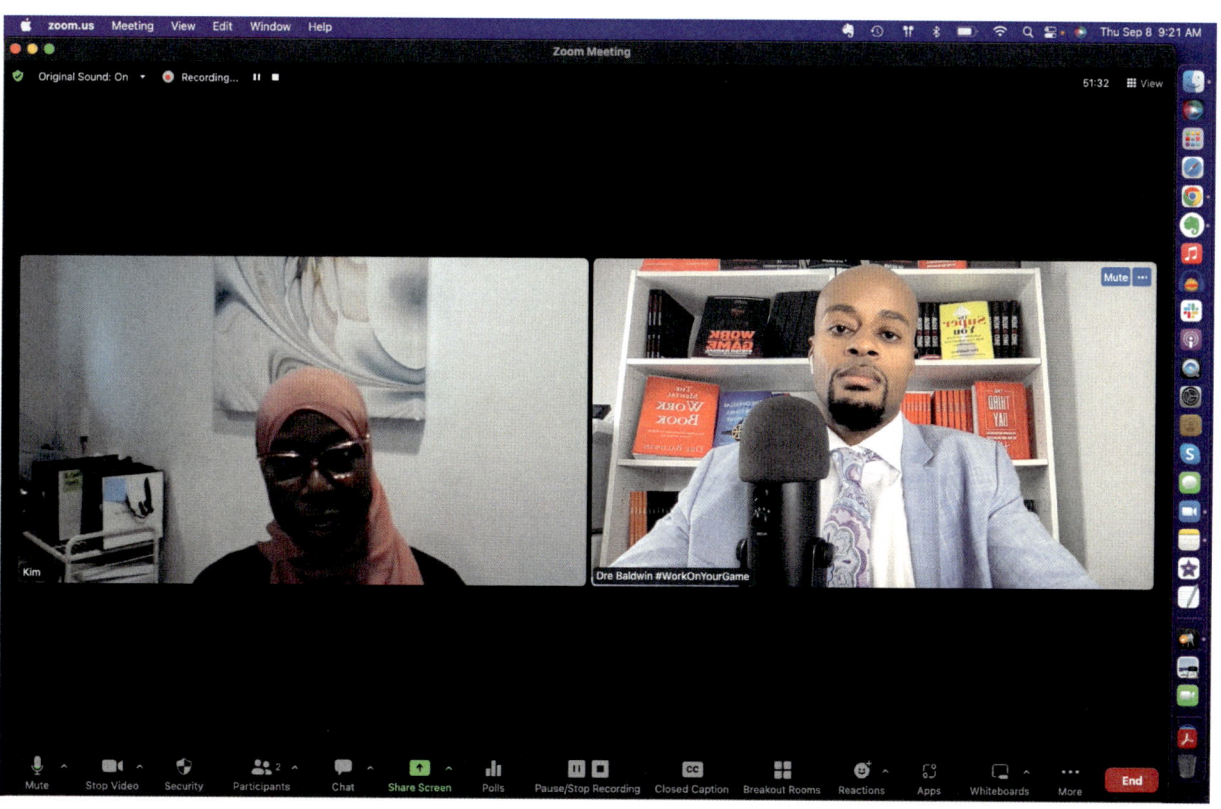

Work On Your Game Inc.
1300 Washington Ave #153
Miami Beach FL 33119

Work On Your Game Inc.
1300 Washington Ave #153
Miami Beach FL 33119

Work On Your Game Inc.
1300 Washington Ave #153
Miami Beach FL 33119

Work On Your Game Inc.
1300 Washington Ave #153
Miami Beach FL 33119

Work On Your Game Inc.
1300 Washington Ave #153
Miami Beach FL 33119

Work On Your Game Inc.
1300 Washington Ave #153
Miami Beach FL 33119

Work On Your Game Inc.
1300 Washington Ave #153
Miami Beach FL 33119

Work On Your Game Inc.
1300 Washington Ave #153
Miami Beach FL 33119

The Third Day
What Separates the Pros from the Amateurs

Dre Baldwin
former NBA Star

The first day of something fun.
- It's *new*. We like new. New is stimulating and exciting.
- We get a chance to show and prove, which can lead to all kinds of benefits.
- You're locked in. We rarely suffer from energy or focus problems at the start of something.

Even the second day still feels new-ish. This new experience hasn't calcified into habit yet.

The human mind and body adapt to things very well, and very quickly. So, around day three, we're already used to this new routine.
- The new car smell novelty is gone. Which means excitement and surface-level motivations are no longer enough to get the job done.
- We can do anything, even hard stuff, once or twice when we know that we'll need to do it *only* once or twice. By day three, we realize: *this is not gonna be all fun and games. There is actual work!*
- If we're not mentally and physically *prepared* for that work, our performance suffers on day three… and only gets worse as time goes on, until or unless we start doing pre-performance prep work that we may or may not be compensated for.
- Everything about what we're doing starts to become routine. When things become routine, we pay less attention to detail. Small bite by small bite, we destroy ourselves from within.

This experience is what I call **The Third Day**.

What is The Third Day?
The Third Day is any situation where the newness and excitement has worn off, there's still much work left to be done, and you are the one who's expected to do it.

- The Third Day can be a day in the middle of your work week or contract project, where it's too far from the beginning to be new, and too far from the end to be excited that it's almost over.
- The Third Day can be a sports practice in the middle of a long season, a practice session that nobody — not even the coaches — wants to be at.
- The Third Day doesn't have to be a *day* - it can be an entire month or year of life, where the work is there to be done, but you would rather be doing *anything else*.

As a mindset and mental approach, The Third Day is your decision to bring your attention to a focus and bring your best effort, even when — *especially when* — you don't quite feel up to it.

This discipline is what truly separates the professionals from the amateurs.
- Not money or contracts.
- Not a job title or a certain level of attention.
- Not the company you work for or the number of followers you've amassed.

A professional is a person who shows up and performs, every single time, regardless of how he/she is feeling.

The Third Day is about how you choose to approach your work, starting with your mental approach.

Why The Third Day Matters
The Third Day matters because, if *talent* was all we needed to become a pro, 75% of current professionals wouldn't be where they are — not because they don't *have* talent, but because there are lots of non-pros who have *more* talent.

If we quit every time we were no longer excited about a project, the world would be filled with incomplete projects and people. And, there are already plenty of both.

You're in the midst of a Third Day right now, and you are quite familiar with the feelings described above.

What to do Now
Reconnect with your focus. Humans are limited to focusing on only one thing at a time. So, Where in your life does being your best, make you one of the best? Put your energy there.

Decide where The Third Day is best utilized for you. You don't need to bring The Third Day Mindset to *everything* you do — that would be mentally and emotionally exhausting — but you do need to decide on the most important areas in which you need to have it. Commit to never wavering in those areas.

Look forward to The Fourth Day. That's the cruise-control ease you feel in your work once you've made it through the toughest of The Third Days. Be forewarned: it won't seem like The Fourth Day will *ever* happen while you're in the midst of The Third Day. But I promise you that it will.

Subscribe to my Work On Your Game Podcast, where every single day I share how you can apply Discipline, Confidence, Mental Toughness and Personal Initiative to your business and life.

#WorkOnYourGame

Work On Your Game Inc.
1300 Washington Ave #153
Miami Beach FL 33119

89

Work On Your Game Inc.
1300 Washington Ave #153
Miami Beach FL 33119

Work On Your Game Inc.
1300 Washington Ave #153
Miami Beach FL 33119

Work On Your Game Inc.
1300 Washington Ave #153
Miami Beach FL 33119

Work On Your Game Inc.
1300 Washington Ave #153
Miami Beach FL 33119

93

Work On Your Game Inc.
1300 Washington Ave #153
Miami Beach FL 33119

Work On Your Game Inc.
1300 Washington Ave #153
Miami Beach FL 33119

Work On Your Game Inc.
1300 Washington Ave #153
Miami Beach FL 33119

Work On Your Game Inc.
1300 Washington Ave #153
Miami Beach FL 33119

Work On Your Game Inc.
1300 Washington Ave #153
Miami Beach FL 33119

Work On Your Game Inc.
1300 Washington Ave #153
Miami Beach FL 33119

Work On Your Game Inc.
1300 Washington Ave #153
Miami Beach FL 33119

Work On Your Game Inc.
1300 Washington Ave #153
Miami Beach FL 33119

Ok… What Do I Do Next?

Do you like what you've read here? Here's what we have for you next…

If you're a high performer who wants to stay at the top of your game, you understand the value of coaching and the strategy and accountability that comes with it. The challenge is in deciding, *who will be that coach, and how can they help ME?*

Knowing this, we've created a FREE guide that will help you apply the mindset & strategies of the world's top 1% of performers and use it to reach the next level in your business.

9 Tools To Apply The Pro Athlete Mindset At Work And Join The Top 1% [So You Can Take a 6-Figure Income To 7]

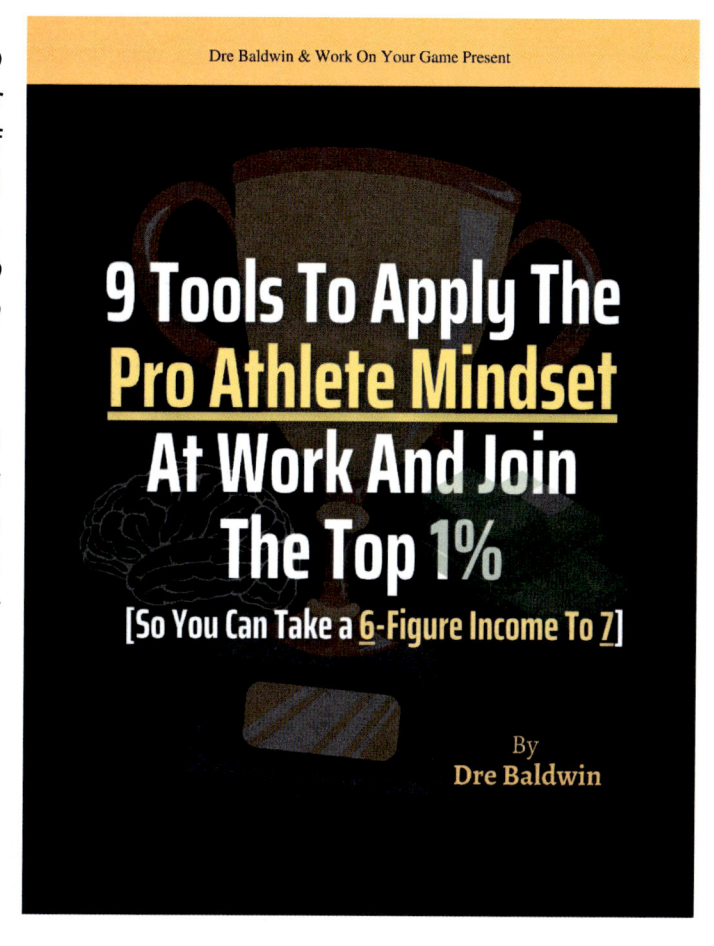

We made this guide for people like you who are serious about playing on their highest level and staying at the highest level. And, we'll mail a FREE physical copy of this guide to your doorstep!

Just email Team@WorkOnMyGame.com with the subject line **Free Coaching Guide** and including your shipping address.

Work On Your Game Inc.
1300 Washington Ave #153
Miami Beach FL 33119

9 Tools To Apply The Pro Athlete Mindset At Work And Join The Top 1% [So You Can Take a 6-Figure Income To 7]

— It will be in the mail and on its way to you!

Here's the website to go to again: www.WorkOnYourGame.com/6AL

We're looking forward to sending it!

On the other hand, if you already **KNOW** we can help you and you're ready to schedule a call to talk about how we can make it happen, go to www.WorkOnYourGame.net/apply and find a time on the calendar that works for you.

Made in the USA
Middletown, DE
02 January 2025